America in Contemporary Fiction

America
in Contemporary
Fiction

by
PERCY H. BOYNTON

NEW YORK
RUSSELL & RUSSELL · INC.
1963

To
THE BOYNTONS
Old and Young

Acknowledgment

Of the following essays those on *Theodore Dreiser, James Branch Cabell,* and *Willa Cather* appeared in original form in my "*Some Contemporary Americans*" (1924); those on *Joseph Hergesheimer, Sherwood Anderson,* and *Sinclair Lewis,* in "*More Contemporary Americans*" (1927). These have been re-written and brought down to the present. The two on the New England novelists, written for this collection, appeared in the "*English Journal*" and the "*New England Quarterly*." The remaining seven are printed here for the first time.

PERCY H. BOYNTON

Contents

(ix)

I

Changing Values

WHEN Henry Adams was trying to satisfy himself as to where mankind was headed, he chose the thirteenth and twentieth centuries as two points in time and studied the forces behind them. Thought, he said, was the highest type of force that affected man; and the curve of changing thought, if shown in a graph after the manner of the physicist, revealed the changing values of men. The line he established ran from unity to multiplicity; from religious order, through scientific inquiry, to economic chaos. The Virgin was supplanted by the dynamo, and the dynamo was in terrific uncontrol. This is in the pseudoscientific metaphor to which he was addicted, and, like any good metaphor, it is suggestive.

Any schoolboy, or anybody with the brains of an average monkey, or anyone with no more ignorance than a statesman, as Henry Adams was always saying, can see at a glance that the history of thought in the United States began in a Colonial period which was direct heir to the thirteenth century, in which God was seated above the apex of an earthly government and in which his will was clear in general if not in detail. And he can see that at the present point on the curve man is perched on a whirling armature of his own invention, wondering if the contrivance can be brought under control.

The average monkey, as endowed by Adams, can also understand that the measure of the value of a man in his day is the measure of envy and admiration in which he is held by the public. He must represent what the average man would like to have—in goods, power, and, most of all, popular esteem. He must be not what the average man hopes to be but what he would like to be if only some miracle could transform him. He must be human enough to have some homely traits and obvious defects of person or character. It is well if he is amiable; but he must be too strong to be very amiable. He must be enviable. All of which is a way of saying that the man who is the measure of human values in his generation does not represent what the generation might advertise as its ideal. He is more of a tacit formula of what youth would like to become, of what elders covet for their children; better embodied than put into words. For example:

The arbitrary but inevitable representative of the seventeenth century is the Puritan churchman-dictator, Cotton Mather up to middle age. He was brought up in a home where his memories were filled with the echoes of biblical speech. He was sent to a college which by statute was founded to equip him to "foil the ould deluder, Satan." The program in this advanced academy, modeled after that of Cambridge University, was modified to promote and reinforce the local Protestant orthodoxy. He learned nothing there of the world he lived in, of his own body and mind, of the social order, of any art but oratory, of any literature as literature, of any foreign language but the dead languages. He was of course allowed to accept from superstition and folklore whatever was wanted to explain the otherwise puzzling ways of man and nature. His followers, after his prompt entry into the pulpit, indorsed him for his partial belief in witchcraft and ignored his partial skepticism. They admired him vaguely for his immense book learning, and more vaguely still for his membership in the Royal Academy.

And for long they deferred to him in church and state. A Calvinist, he regarded life as a preparation for an afterlife, accepted the burden of man's first sin and the vengeance of an angry god, lived in dread of eternal punishment for his natural depravity, and yearned to be of the elect who were assured of salvation. As a citizen he had no doubts. He knew that he was of the elect: born and bred to govern.

He was practical and efficient in politics. His mind may have derived a peculiar quality, as Macaulay affirmed of the Puritan, from the daily contemplation of superior beings and eternal interests; but it was also affected by daily controversy. He could nod sagely at John Winthrop's acknowledgment that a hostile move at the English court had been blocked "through the Lord's good providence, and the care of our friends in England." He was aware that three thousand miles of salt water were a useful barrier behind which he could protest his loyalty to the king and disregard him as far as he dared. Mastery at home was another matter. The rights invoked against the crown were highly objectionable when asserted against the government of Massachusetts. The only way out for this godly insubordinate was to appeal to scriptural authority for monarchical control and to quote his grandfather, John Cotton: "Democracy I do not conceyve that ever God did ordain as a fit government eyther for church or commonwealth. If the people be governors, who shall be governed?"

As an ecclesiastic he was even more frankly dictator. He barred from church membership all whose views or behavior disqualified them in his judgment, and he refused to let them worship by themselves. He agreed with Nathaniel Ward as to the folly of the doctrine that men should enjoy liberty of conscience: "Let all the wits under the Heavens lay their heads together and find an assertion worse than this and I will petition to be chosen universal Ideot of the World." He had his legal machinery at hand for use against offenders, and, living in a cruel age in the fear of a cruel god, he played his cruel role in the passionate conviction of all dictators that his plan was a plan of salvation, that it must be made to succeed at all costs, and that the perverse must take it or take the consequences.

Like men of his kind he was better at controlling others than at self-control. He was quick to wrath. He could vent his temper on an offender if an offender was at hand, and he could quarrel openly and noisily with other pillars of church and state. He was a feaster as well as a faster, and a mercilessly possessive master of a succession of wives. He was carnal, acquisitive, avid of power—a man whom there were few to love. But there were many to praise him, for he was the logical product of his generation.

Cotton Mather stood at the forefront until the turn of the eighteenth century. In the name of the Lord he took what his little world had to give him, and until his world turned against him he was a preeminently enviable man. Yet his world did turn away from him. In 1662, the year before he was born, Michael Wigglesworth's rhymed tract, *The*

Day of Doom, appeared. It was the most popular work of the times. In 1728, when Mather died, Benjamin Franklin was a young man on the way toward publishing the first American book to rival *The Day of Doom* in popular appeal. It was entitled *The Way to Wealth*.

Franklin was the first national character both to secede from Puritanism and to challenge the religious life by the secular. Brought up "piously, in the dissenting way," he had many of the traits of his ancestry. He shared the Puritans' will-to-power, though he exercised power with a benignity that was no part of their Calvinism. He shared their belief in self-discipline, but kept his temper better; and he took no stock in asceticism as an end in itself. In his thrift and efficiency he was so like his parents that he could draw a lesson from them in the epitaph he compiled and could couple industry with faith in the injunction to

> Be encouraged to diligence in thy calling
> And distrust not Providence.

He believed, as Winthrop did, that the Lord helped them that helped themselves, but he differed from Winthrop and Mather, at least in candor, by consistently listing Providence in second place. It was Mather's "Essays To Do Good" that Franklin quoted rather than any of his sermons. He rarely referred to the Bible.

Franklin's self-schooling set him off at a tangent from Mather's orbit. In his teens he was absorbing Xenophon and Plutarch, Bunyan, Burton and Defoe, Locke and Shaftesbury, Addison and Pope. He had no interest in the classics except to discount their value in education, but he acquired a reading knowledge of French, Italian, and Spanish. His most sustained study was in physical and natural science. And the best of his education came from sources that Mather never tapped: travel and contact with superior minds. All this did much toward making him a citizen of the world and more toward making him a practical master of various tools for use in a busy life. He was not living in an antechamber to heaven. If other folks regarded it so, he still saw need for a lot of additions and improvements. To make these he wanted "useful attainments." He escaped being a poet, he stated, but prose writing was useful to him. There are almost no references in his autobiography to theater, drama, fiction, music, painting, sculpture, architecture. There is no instinctive resort in his writings to the illuminative facts and principles of history or the broad reaches of philosophy, and he seldom referred even to the wider implications of science. Comparison of Franklin's range of interests

with those of Burke or Talleyrand or Jefferson, or of
his fellow-townsman Francis Hopkinson, exposes its
limitations. Use loomed large; enjoyment, hardly
at all.

Use was the end of education, and use was the
measure of religion. He conceded that the church
was an effective ethical stabilizer for such as needed
it. He believed that there was a God and that the
most effective service to him was in social usefulness. He believed in immortality and a system of
present or future rewards and punishments, for he
said these concepts were necessary to any religion.
He paid an annual church subscription as an indorsement of the "propriety and utility of public
worship when rightly conducted." He was willing
even to tolerate the New England orthodoxy which
would not tolerate his deism.

His interest in means and ends, from youth up, led
him to the use of practical psychology, especially in
the technique of not rousing opposition. He employed it in politics and in statesmanship. He knew
that the public was moved by passion, prejudice,
local interest, personal selfishness. "In matters of
general concern to the people, and especially where
burdens are to be laid on them, it is of use to consider, as well what they will be apt to think and
say, as what they ought to think." With Chester-
fieldian urbanity he kept his head clear and his

temper unruffled. When he was hardest pushed he could joke, or juggle a phrase, or turn a neat evasion, or strike out a slogan. "Give me liberty or give me death" was not bad for an eloquent Patrick Henry, but Franklin's colloquial "We must all hang together, or we'll all hang separately" was even better, and could be quoted in any mood.

His practical canniness was at the back of his success. To middle life he was the good journalist and resourceful inventor, both types thriving on quickness to apply ideas to social demands. There was little of the contemplative in him except as he contemplated contrivances and organizations. Before he was fifty he had freed himself from the need of daily earning; he had founded an academy, a journal, a debating club, a philosophical society, a circulating library. He had devised the lightning rod, invented a stove, improved street illumination and fire-fighting. He had held public office from justice of the peace to postmaster-general. One accepts it as a normal performance for Franklin that he founded the longest-lived periodical in American history and the favorite almanac of the period.

But more than this was needed to make Franklin the enviable man of his day: He was completely representative of his America. Any youth of small beginnings could aspire to his success and no man of privilege could look down on it. And he was in-

comparably dramatized: Franklin entering Philadelphia with the rolls under his arms; Franklin in his
examination before Parliament; Franklin with kite
and key in the thunderstorm; Franklin with scratch
wig and woolen stockings at the French court.
Hardly a man of his century but Voltaire was center
of so many familiar tableaux; none but Dr. Johnson
was so endearingly homely withal. And in the popular heart he had the advantage of them both. He
did not stab like Voltaire or bully like Johnson, and
he was safely between the two in his views—up to
date, perhaps a bit ahead of his generation, but not
too far. Toward the end of his career he once lagged
a step behind. The Constitutional Convention had
been long at work with waning hopes of success.
One day Franklin took the floor to say that the task
seemed too great for human powers. Would it not
be wise to open the sessions with prayer? His motion was defeated, and the Constitution took shape
without the aid or the mention of God—not even of
Franklin's unorthodox God of the deists. Practical
efficiency won the day. Americans liked Franklin
better for that than for any belated devoutness.

Mather lived and moved on the assumption that
he was God's deputy; that his task as a churchman
was to bring the assurance of salvation to the elect,
the conviction of sin to the damned; and as a secular

aristocrat to insure the performance of his will on earth. Franklin, frankly worldly, retained certain of the idioms of godliness, freed himself from lust for money by getting all he wanted, and served his Deity by working for a sane, comfortable, efficient democracy. Before the American experiment was fifty years old a new formula was needed for the indorsement of the rugged individualist who still talked of God's will while he piled up a fortune by exploiting land in the West and labor in the East. He was christened Empire Builder, Instrument of America's Manifest Destiny.

"We have," John Adams wrote in 1808, "one material which actually constitutes an aristocracy that governs the nation. That material is wealth. Talents, birth, virtues, services, sacrifices are of little consideration with us." In the years to follow, two phrases were to gain growing currency: "from the Log Cabin to the White House" for the President, and "born of poor but honest parents" for the captain of finance. The military hero could still be hurrahed as Andrew Jackson was, but the popular model was coming to be the builder of a great fortune. The ideal of democracy was to start with equal opportunity but to end with a maximum of privilege, property, and the power that lies in the persuasive influence of a long purse, an oblique eye, and an open hand. The most popular American au-

thor of the period paid homage to the most picturesque of the self-made men, in the volume signed
by Washington Irving and devoted to John Jacob
Astor.

Astor began, according to Irving, "on the nar-
rowest scale"; but he was endowed with an imposing array of traits which included not only industry,
economy, integrity, and an "aspiring spirit that always looked upward," but also "a sagacity quick to
grasp and convert every circumstance to its advantage," and no end of self-confidence. When he entered the western fur business, he found the field
occupied by a strong and well-intrenched company.
As he needed powerful support, he offered, "if aided
and protected by government to turn the whole of
that trade into American channels." Aid was prom-
ised and a charter was secured. The capital was his
own and so was the organization, "for, though he
had a board of directors, they were merely nominal
. . . . he preferred the imposing and formidable aspect of a corporation."

At this point in the chronicle Irving dimly recognized the need of justifying the patron who had
amply subsidized the use of his biographer's prestige. The formula was ready to hand: The fur magnate deserved the gratitude of his less predatory fel-
low-countrymen because he and his like "by their
great commercial enterprise have enriched nations,

peopled wildernesses, and extended the bounds of empire." Astor had spoken in these terms himself, and Irving quoted him with abundance of italics: "*Our enterprise is grand and deserves success, and I hope in God it will meet it*. If my object was merely gain of money, I should say, think whether it is best to save what we can, and abandon the place; *but the very idea is like a dagger in my heart*." The project had its ups and downs under both Providence and the government; but in the end the "venerable projector . . . . had the satisfaction of knowing, ere his eyes closed upon the world, that the flag of his country again waved over ASTORIA."

A portrait depends on the man who makes it. James Truslow Adams has recently supplied not a painting but a set of snapshots, untouched.

"Astor had been a foreign immigrant, scarcely able to read and write, yet there he was, rich as Croesus, and dictating to the government.

"Astor was czar in the Far Northwest fur trade, where his power was greater than that of the Federal government.

"Astor in New York, what with his fur trading, his city real estate, and deals of one sort or another, was setting the pace.

"When the first Astor died in 1848, the $20,000,-000 fortune left by him was a milestone in American financial and social history."

In his day the Empire Builder could commandeer what he wanted—a dummy board of directors, "the imposing and formidable aspect of a corporation," government indorsement, or the pen of the most popular writer in the land. And by this writer, who may safely be accepted as spokesman for his public, Astor was canonized as a figure to revere in the religion of Mammon whose capital city was New York and whose new empire was the United States of America.

What the findings of science did to philosophy, in the half-century after Astor's death, and what the application of science did to life, are commonplaces of history. But society surrenders more readily to the inventor than to the philosopher. Idioms of action are more mobile than idioms of thought and speech. Maxwell and Marconi and the Wright brothers and the maker of the gasoline engine swept to victory in an America which was still well intrenched against Marx and Darwin. So the fortune-makers, who were indebted to the machine for their wealth, were ostentatious not only in spending it but also in pursuit of the new fashion of expiatory benevolence and in service as bulwarks of the church. For a man of Theodore Roosevelt's temper this presented a nice problem.

He was the proud citizen of a land in which a

divinely ordained economic system was conserved against all foes by the Republican party; and he was reinforced in his conviction by pulpit and press. A Brooklyn clergyman declaimed that the Democratic platform of 1896 was made in hell. The *New York Tribune* explained after election that Bryan had been defeated because right was right and God was God. But the situation was confusing; there were abuses within the system, and even the men Roosevelt chose to describe as "malefactors of great wealth" were appealing to God. It was proper enough for President McKinley to "pray for light and guidance" before evolving a Rooseveltian imperialistic program; but it was embarrassing when Baer, the mine operator, defied Roosevelt and the public with the declaration that "God in his Infinite Wisdom had given control of the property interests of the country" into the right hands. The problem for Roosevelt was to wage a holy war in behalf of the existing order, carrying it in two directions. He must fight malefactors from within, and he must overwhelm "all the lunatics, all the idiots, all the knaves, all the cowards, all the honest people who are slow-witted"—all the people of every stripe who condemned themselves by voting the opposition tickets. Business and righteousness were in eternal alliance; if they were not, they ought to be; at any rate he was the Conscience of Big Business.

(15)

To conduct this war he was equipped with a confessed ignorance of economics, a wavering policy, a love of conflict, an assertive sense of righteousness, and a stunning capacity for showmanship.

But these characteristics, even with his showmanship, could not have made him the enviable man if he had not been regarded as a moral champion of popular causes. In the cause of the people against the double menace of financial buccaneers and political radicals, the records show that he was painfully uncertain as to policies and tactics, sometimes because his ideas were muddled and sometimes because he saw that political discretion was the better part of valor and avoided or postponed issues. They show further that his liberal programs were often adopted from the Bryan whom he had once compared to the "leaders of the Terror of France in mental and moral attitude." And they show that no Republican could surpass his fear of ultra-liberal doctrines. When he was objurgating Bryan, the boy orator was as bad as Debs, a menace to the nation. When he was at outs with E. H. Harriman, he outlawed the railroad man by calling him "at least as undesirable a citizen as Debs, or Moyer, or Haywood." This was good popular tactics. Each decade has its abusive epithet for the liberals and a way of identifying it with everything villainous. It was what the Federalists did a hundred

years earlier when they damned a man by calling
him a republican. Roosevelt stood like a Colossus,
fending off the wrong people on the right wing and
all the people on the left wing with the same salvo
of abuse for both. It was spectacular and effective.

So was his role as imperialist. McKinley, after
prayer, had seen his way to a new program of offensive and defensive policies. Roosevelt followed it as
McKinley never would have done. "I seized the ca-
nal" he declared in one of his indiscreet moments.
Subsequently the government paid $25,000,000 con-
science money; but it was a popular move. Arbitration should prevail among nations except where national honor was involved—as it always was; but a
big navy was better than a board of arbitration.
"Speak softly and carry a big stick, you will go
far," he quoted from an African proverb. Nothing
is more revealing as to the selective memories of
T. R. and the American people. "Carry a big stick"
was all that either remembered. And the people
doted on him for it.

As the years went on he appealed more and more
successfully to the Anglo-Saxon love of a moral
principle that is identified with material interests.
He was champion of the square deal, dispenser of
substantial justice, trust-buster; political knight-
errant against naughty rich men, malignant poor
men, despoilers of the national honor, foreign ag-

(17)

gressors; excoriator of muckrakers, nature-fakers, members of the Ananias Club. He was the sportsman-hunter-soldier. He would disinherit any son who would not accept a broken bone for the honor of a place on the Harvard eleven. He was presidential huntsman, careful to have the honor of shooting the first bear. He left the White House for the wilds of Africa. He came back to stand at Armageddon and battle for the Lord. He smashed the wicked Republican party singing "Onward Christian Soldiers," and returned to the fold after the disaster because it was the only practical thing to do; there were no loaves and fishes to hold a third party together. When he finally came round to the idea of American entry into the World War, his application to supply a division of infantry was refused by men who naturally feared that if he were given the chance he would run away with the show.

And Americans idolized him because he was so essentially their man. He was the first President within living memory who had not been enveloped in official dignity; the only one for whom a nursery toy was ever named. They reveled in a leader whom John Morley could in one mood describe as a combination of St. Vitus and St. Paul and in another could compare to Niagara Falls. They shared his satisfaction with the general economic situation and his solicitudes for it. They had just been aroused by

the war with Spain and shared his militant nation-
alism. They could understand his explosive talk.
"I have to use bromides in my business," he ex-
plained in confidence. And they swarmed to his sup-
port as a crusader, wielder of the sword of the Lord.
His place in the hearts of the people survived his
loss of power. From the day he entered the White
House till the day of his death no other man in the
United States was quite so enviable to the average
American.

However, the war was fought not by soldiers of
the Lord but by inventors, engineers, and craftsmen
who made and used the machines of their contriv-
ing. It was the machines that ran away with the
show and that ran still faster when the show was
over. The law of the machine was supreme in the
East where the machines—including the machinery
of finance—were made and operated. A Nebraskan
staged the last great rally of old-fashioned godliness
against the advance of science; a Texan drafted a
constitutional amendment in the name of old-fashioned moralism, and a Minnesotan sponsored the
enforcement act. A Quaker President from Iowa via
California never stopped coupling rugged individualism of the Astor type with spiritual values,
while he speeded up the machine till it ran off the
road and into the ditch. And when it crashed it be-

came clear that it could not be moralized or spiritualized or theologized into running-order again. People stopped saying "God save the commonwealth" and began talking about planned production to the same end.

That is what terminates the curve of thought in the United States today with such a dramatic interrogation point. Up to now the people have always had something to believe in, and from time to time some one to look to as an embodiment of that belief: the power of faith, the power of social efficiency, the power of manifest destiny, the power of a righteous existing order. A reading of representative American novelists reveals at length the quandary in which America finds itself.

II

Two New England Regionalists

IN 1936 Maine and Vermont were the only states
in the Union to vote the Republican ticket, the
only antifederalist states who put their backs
up and played rebel by clinging to a party label
which for generations had stood for what they were
now fighting against. A hundred and fifty years
before, Massachusetts and then Connecticut went
down in vain opposition to Jeffersonian democracy
in a last stand of the Old Guard. Maine was then a
district of Massachusetts, not admitted to statehood
until 1820; and Vermont, judging from Connecticut
historians, was largely peopled from the Nutmeg
State—no state itself until 1791.

So the youngest of the New England common-
wealths, Maine as described by Mary Ellen Chase
and Vermont as described by Dorothy Canfield
Fisher, came honestly by their insurgency which
looked so much like conservatism. They are more
"native" than their neighbors, as one can see by
comparing the student rolls at Bowdoin and the
University of Maine, Middlebury and the University of Vermont, with those of Amherst and Har-

vard, Wesleyan and Yale. And they are less urban in their makeup. Neither has a large city today, and they are well off the highroad between New York and Boston. Maine is the last state in New England to depend chiefly on the sea; it is still mostly woodland. Vermont is mostly mountain—the only state in the country to ballast its railroad tracks and pave its sidewalks with marble. And both at present are deeply disturbed at being converted by city folk into summer paradises and skeeing resorts, adopted and occupied by aliens. "Broadway in Maine" and Bennington College, Vermont, do not belong there. They have been "fetched in" by outsiders who menace the communities by fetching in yet more outsiders who will buy up the best building sites but never partake of the cultural traditions.

Miss Chase has written a retrospective book, *A Goodly Heritage*, to show what the old days bequeathed to the men and women of twentieth-century Maine—a heritage they need to fall back on in these less heroic times. In the beginnings of English occupation, Maine was all coast and backwoods and is mostly divided between them even yet. So the coast first determined the life of the province. It was a stable life, though derived from the unstable sea. The fishers were always going away, but were always homeward bound, whether they went no farther than the banks or as far as Captain Ahab in

quest of whales. The fishers brought home sustenance and the merchants brought not only goods
but a cosmopolitan experience which enriched the
little ports as much as the provender did.

Both fishers and shippers built their own craft, or
had them built near home, and in those days when
the exercise of craftsmanship was untrammeled by
unions they turned their skill also to building on
shore: barns and sheds, stores and taverns, dwell-
ing-houses, schoolhouses, meeting-houses. They
could carve as well as saw, too, and their skill remains in many a doorway, capital, and molding
ashore, as well as in many a figurehead on the sea.
The beauty and strength of the villages was made
by the hands of the shipbuilders, whose building of
boats, which combined grace and sturdiness, was a
matter of life and death to the men who used them.
So the goodly heritage of Maine includes integrity
of workmanship, resourcefulness, courage, a love of
beauty that does not talk about itself but is no less
genuine for that, and an amplitude of spirit which is
the inevitable fruit of meeting primitive dangers and
encountering all sorts and conditions of men.

Conscious of this heritage, Miss Chase has written definitely as a regionalist, from first word to last
between the end papers with their coastal scenes.
Her theme is the vanished past of the Pine Tree
State. To bring it through the generations down to

the present she has written chronicle novels: *Mary Peters*, about Mary, her father, her husband, her son; *Silas Crockett*, about Silas and his forebears. The life and character of the port and the life and character of the men who build it up only to see it swept away by an industrial tide, the replacement of the clipper ships by passenger steamers and speed boats, of shipyards by truck gardens and filling stations, the buying-up of the men of power by the comfort-seekers—these are the warp of her stories. And the outcomes are the outcomes of industrial revolution, not the denouements of well-made plots. Tales drawn from such material may make good novels if, as in Miss Chase's adroit hands, the characters are well drawn and honestly followed through surrounding circumstances.

Just how clumsy such novels could become in the days when plots had to dominate and the conventional plot elements were conscientiously lugged in is demonstrated in an earlier Maine novel, Mrs. Stowe's *The Pearl of Orr's Island*. The Pearl is an orphan cast up on the coast, destined from the first storm to be a heroine of conventional romance. Her hero is a native son who becomes a successful sea captain in very young manhood. The obstacle between them is a mildly predatory hussy who ensnares the hero, loses him, and eventually delivers him to the exemplary and self-effacing Pearl whose

identity is laboriously connected with an early love
of the village parson. The human element is drawn
from Maine in the 1860's; the plot elements are all
to be found in medieval romance; the product is
what one might expect. Miss Chase might have
written in that mode if, so to speak, she had been
her own grandmother. But writing in the twentieth century, she demonstrates her own gifts, while
illustrating the gains in narrative technique that
have been made in the last two generations. The
reasons for Miss Chase's greater effectiveness are
twofold. One is that modern dialogue, description,
characterization, depend more on development from
within, tell their own story, refrain from the eager
exposition made needless by greater narrative skill.
The other is that Miss Chase is not an adopted
daughter of Maine, like Mrs. Stowe, but is to the
manner born. As a consequence she presents characters, particularly her women, as they act and talk,
assuming truthfully that they are natural, not glee-
fully hinting that they are queer, quaint, and amusing. It is the difference between the skill of the real
raconteur and the maladroitness of the jocose story-
teller who jeopardizes his effect by promising his
hearers the funniest thing they ever heard. This
deftness in narrative and characterization is exercised to its highest degree in Miss Chase's beautiful
Dawn in Lyonnesse, which, however, is not a region-
al tale and so is not germane to this discussion.

America in Contemporary Fiction

Miss Chase in *Mary Peters* and *Silas Crockett* has written novels, but she has also supplied documents for the student who will one day compile his dissertation on "The Effects of the Industrial Revolution on the American Frontier." John Henry, Herculean laborer, literally broke his heart competing with the machine—in the railroad version with a steam drill, and in the river-levee version with a steam crane. Mike Fink, king of the keelboatmen, was driven off the water by the stern-wheeler. The Maine sailor and boatbuilder have succumbed to steam and steel. With such material the novelist can do little but record the lives of the victims before the march of progress. Miss Chase presents the survival of human character and the immolation of human life and points no moral to adorn her tales. Nevertheless, the moral, or inner implication, is never lost. Man is trying to cope with himself, with his neighbors and competitors, and with the natural and supernatural forces surrounding him. Once the supernatural forces were the powers behind wind and wave; but there came a time when a man-made demon could defy wind and wave and, doing so, could sweep out of its way wooden ships and shipbuilders, sails and sailors, with a contrivance that reduced the wind to a casual and minor factor in navigation.

Steam also reduced many an old shipmaster to the

point at which he could no longer afford to live in the family homestead so that, like Captain Peters, he could in his later years only send his son to inspect and report on its condition. And the son, reluctantly obedient, found it fenced, with wide lawns, formal gardens, a golf course in the former meadow, the barn a garage, and at the door a butler politefully regretful that in the absence of the purchaser he could not admit the man who had been born and bred there. The residence was intact and immaculate, restored and re-equipped, but the Peters family, to whom it once was a home, were stranded outside.

Dorothy Canfield Fisher, invincible Vermonter, has had a drought to record instead of a hurricane. Vermont crumbles but is not wrecked. In all her stories, Vermont character is asserting itself more or less vainly to oppose irresistible forces. The success of the resistance is never included in the stories, but it is usually implied at the end as the obvious theme of an unwritten sequel. Slow crumbling is too vague to submit to chronicle treatment; it needs reinforcement by plot structure, and Mrs. Fisher has her constant factors for this plot: a native Vermonter who has strayed away from home, been distracted by wealth, and dazzled by European sophistication, preserves his integrity by taking refuge in the old ways of self-fulfilment as a hill villager. In *Rough Hewn* the Boy, after showing promise as a New York business bandit, takes a year off to find himself in travel, and finding the Girl astray in Europe, the daughter of American expatriates, returns with her to take up life at the old family sawmill. In *The Brimming Cup* the Vermont story is projected against an earlier European background. In *The Bent Twig* the girl of the right stock rejects a rich young tomcat and is bewildered by a wealthy aunt who almost estranges her from the family, and by an art broker who almost alienates her from the elect Native Son. He, in turn, has inherited Colorado mines, which he gives back to the workers, and the lovers retire to his home acres and a reforestation project.

Better than these, and most effective of Mrs. Fisher's output, is *Bonfire*. The formula persists, but it is overwhelmed by the human elements in the tale. The central factor this time is not an individual but the composite personality of the village. This is taciturn toward strangers, loquacious when uninvaded, capable of the most extreme group reactions under excitement and of every sort of personal eccentricity in times of peace. Mrs. Fisher describes its behavior when the village doctor scandalizes it by marrying a girl of dubious character from "the Shelf," an upland hillside slum:

Two New England Regionalists

"The first reaction of Clifford people to Doctor Anson's marriage and all that went with it was a reflex group response such as follows an earthquake or a flood—something that happens to all as much as to one. No matter what their individual temperaments, they all cried out the same things when they talked, held their tongues by instinct on the same occasions. For, of course, even the children knew enough to shut their mouths during the few days when detectives, newspaper reporters and other prying outsiders were around, vainly looking for clews. . . . . No other silence about Doctor Craft's marriage was kept in Clifford than the little oasis of it about his sister. . . . . It was felt that self-control need go no further. In fact talk and plenty of it was called for. To exclaim and condemn was right and proper. . . . . As it was, the fire of disapproval . . . . presently began to burn itself out. The stronger souls . . . . emerging a little from collective mob feeling, began out of sheer boredom . . . . occasionally to turn the conversation to something else. . . . . People went back to their own naturally different ways of looking at life."

These different ways are the theme of the book's opening pages, in which one by one thumbnail sketches of the dramatis personae are given: Sherwin Dewy, nature lover and homely philosopher, and Sherwin Dewy's dog; Mr. Lawrence Stewart, keeper of a museum, his own perfect ancestral home, and Lawrence Stewart's cat; Father Kirby, the ascetic rector; the elderly Kemp sisters, inseparable in their difference; the Deans, the Merrills, the Nyes; the elect, who lived on The Street; the lower middle class, though never so described, who lived at Clifford's Four Corners; the folks beyond the pale on Searles' Shelf. All these were to react to Doctor Craft, gifted and restless young physician, and to Miss Anna, his sister, who had just returned from a year in Paris to her visiting nurse's round in the township. And all were to be affected by the subtly seductive presence of Lixlee Burdick, the Searles' Shelf girl, who could take on the ways of politer society, who was too lovely of skin and hair and contour, and who was a perennial type of amoral carnality which found its perfect hunting ground in a tidy New England village. In the end she changed life for almost everyone she passed. She turned the heads of all the men, she estranged the women, and by the forces she set in motion she united the doctor's sister and the rector in holy matrimony, captured old Mr. Stewart in the bonds of unholy wedlock, drove Isabel Foote into effective professional life, handed a rich and eligible husband to Olivia Merrill, even by indirection founded a co-operative home for the poor upland children who were impossibly far from school.

Two New England Regionalists

In all this there is none of the play of economic forces that are so devastating to Maine and its people. The only machine in the novel, the locomotive, annually brings and takes away the alien city dwellers who do not care to know and are not permitted to see the inner life of the village. The story goes back of the machine to the vulnerable nature of Man. Lixlee is the serpent in the Garden of Eden and she is Eve after her talk with the serpent. She is original sin in a Calvinistic hamlet playing upon the natural depravity of the townsfolk. Life is unfertilized there, or unfortified, by the contact of the seamen with the outer world. A few who have fared forth save their souls, but the many are nearer to the native instinct of Sherwin Dewey's dog, which belongs in the wilds, and of Lawrence Stewart's cat, which has disreputable relations with a rover from the woods. It is a real distinction between Mrs. Fisher's characters and Miss Chase's; and it is a distinction which accounts for disintegration rather than noble defeat. *Bonfire* seems the truest of the Vermont stories because it is not complicated by Mrs. Fisher's loyalty to Vermont. For once she does not conclude with the implication that the leading characters are finally on the verge of living happily ever after. This tale ends with Anna Craft's observation that life teaches one a good deal, and with her confession when queried that she can't quite make up her mind what the lesson is.

In *Seasoned Timber*, however, Mrs. Fisher has been carried along by the tide of events. The change is from absorption in Vermont character as a product of the past to vindication of Vermont character as a bulwark against the present. And it is also, explicitly, a change from instinctive allusion to Henry James, recurrent in the earlier works, to inevitable allusion to Sinclair Lewis. For in this latest novel Mrs. Fisher declares with a sober face what Lewis has declared with his tongue in his cheek, that fascist materialism, leading to Yahoo, Black Legion savagery, "can't happen here" in Vermont. She acknowledges at last that Vermont, like Maine, is losing its basic resources. "Sheep have gone; granite and marble are giving way to synthetic materials; woodenware, to metal; woolens, to the pressure of southern wage-scales." Vermont has one final defence—its native backbone. Henry James cannot help her in this crisis; but she is so conscious of her new ally that in the midst of a caricature of George Clarence Wheaton, a magnified Babbitt, she interpolates, "Really Sinclair Lewis is a phongraph record! When you read him you think he's laying it on too thick. Not at all. He doesn't exaggerate a hair." Mrs. Fisher, too, lays it on thick in the anti-fascist propaganda which dominates the latter part of the novel, but in the long approach to this she continues in the more nearly Jamesian fashion of her more nearly America-European novels. The result- ant product is a hybrid but an interesting one, with its appeals to popular response from various types of reader: the people who love Vermont, the people who love any kind of localism, the people who love nature, the people who love a love story, the people who love noble sentiments, the people who hate bigotry of any sort and anti-Semitism in particular. It is effective argument, though as art it suffers by comparison with *Bonfire*.

Obviously, such old-fashioned, retrospective ma- terial as all this does not call for and should not adopt modern, or modernistic, treatment. It would be silly and fantastic to fit out George Eliot from Katherine Mansfield's wardrobe. Miss Chase prop- erly resorts in her chronicles to direct, extended nar- rative—a narrative which explains more than it dramatizes—and develops specific episodes more for the drawing of character than for the heightening of plot. There are few moments of tension. The tales move on as the years move on. If the mem- bers of the seafaring families meditate or speculate, Miss Chase sets their thoughts in order and restates them. Thus the old, old stories are told in the old, old ways. Mrs. Fisher, with her dependence on plot, dramatizes more freely and frequently employs a vivid event or an emotional scene. But when she uses these devices, if that is the proper term for them, she uses them in established ways, except as she shows the steadily improving narrative technique of making the passages self-sufficient and self-explanatory. She secures her effects in old ways brought down to date, not in new ways.

Both novelists present New England in true and faithful pictures. But neither singly nor together do they give the whole picture, for as I suggested at the outset they deal only with the two states which so neatly registered themselves in opposition not only to the rest of the country but to the rest of their own provincial region. It would be idle to list all the aspects of the region that are not included in the novels of Miss Chase and Mrs. Fisher; but there is one that demands a word—the Puritanism of New England and its vestigial remains. Mrs. Fisher and Miss Chase have not been primarily concerned with Puritanism; those who have done so must have a separate discussion; but they have woven it into their narratives just as the ordinary New Englanders of Maine and Vermont have woven it into the fabric of their lives. Their picture of the rural New England scene is the better for it, an autumnal picture in which the old order of upland Vermont and seaboard Maine have little to do but face the gathering winter of their discontent.

III

Puritanism in New England

IN THE decade from 1850 to 1860 barriers between the older regions of the country were broken down by the development of what was then thought of as rapid transportation. At last one could go from Boston to New York, even from Boston to Albany, in a single day. That explains why Harriet Beecher Stowe opened both *The Minister's Wooing* in 1857 and *Oldtown Folks* in 1869 with references to "pre-railroad times." Writing in the post–Civil War period she chose to describe New England life of the post–Revolutionary War period. Her historical facts can be checked against the earlier times, but the atmosphere of the tales was that of her own day, and truly so, for pre-railroad ways of living survived well past the middle of the nineteenth century. A Beecher herself, acquainted with Connecticut, Maine, and Massachusetts, and enabled for a few years to contemplate New England from the vantage point of Cincinnati, Ohio, she was a competent witness as to the merits and shortcomings of the home folk. And her novels still make good reading, not so much for her plots, which are always imposed on her materials, as for the veracity of character, episode, and social background and for the critical soundness of her observations on them.

What her mind harked back to in her best writing period was the little theocracy of the Pilgrims and the Puritans in which for long the ministers were the only nobility; in which *Christo et ecclesiae* was the natural motto for the first college; and in which the average villagers were schooled in theology, ready in echoing its phrases and even in coping with its involutions. She realized that this intellectual discipline produced more strength and purity than happiness and that it was often crushing to the weaker souls. She knew that the doctrines based on the teachings of Jesus worked best in a vacuum, that leading "professors" were openly false to them, and that the preacher who applied them too definitely and insistently was liable to pay for his urgency with the loss of his pulpit. So whether his creed was Calvinism, Arminianism, or New Divinity, the average preacher was more zealous as a logician than as a sympathetic pastor of his flock.

Naturally, in such a social order irreligion sprang up among the young collegians, as she acknowledged; and, as the noxious doctrines were most aggressively propounded in France and bore the most poisonous fruits there, Francophobia was one of the results she recognized. Yet withal she believed stoutly that the old Puritan discipline of mind and conduct, and the old integrities which it fortified, formed the best foundations for a new order in which "monarchy, aristocracy and theocracy, with their peculiar trains of ideas, were passing away, and New England was coming within the sweep of pure republican influences, in which the individual is everything." The significance of this was the greater because she twice referred to New England, and she meant Colonial, Puritan New England, as "the seed-bed of this great American Republic."

Elizabeth Stuart Phelps's *The Gates Ajar*, an almost exact contemporary of *Oldtown Folks*, is a miniature on a special thesis—not salvation but the nature of heaven. An aunt and a niece, bereft of husband and brother, speculate at length. The older woman is a true flower of New England. "A woman who knows something about fate, freewill and foreknowledge absolute, who is not ignorant of politics and talks intelligently of Agassiz's latest fossil, who can understand a German quotation, and has heard of Strauss and Neander, who can dash her sprightliness against [the] dry bones of metaphysics and theology, yet never speak an accent above [an] essentially woman's voice," this blue-stocking theologian meets all comers in defending her thesis of a material heaven with a sublimated but still corporeal population, and both gives and receives much consolation from the thought. The little book was a very popular theological tract among a generation who were much more recent than they seem. Miss Phelps's heaven was unorthodox in conception, but it was a familiar, cozy place, and the amiable tone of her unorthodoxy was thrown into relief against the grim aridity of the faithful whose idea of eternal bliss and how to earn it was only a degree more primitive than hers.

Mrs. Deland's *John Ward, Preacher* attracted such a reading in its day (1888) that it is worth mention if only as an index to popular taste and a contrast to her novel of 1911 *The Iron Woman*. *John Ward*, the first novel of a young writer, is sentimental melodrama of the most conventional type. Ward, an iron-bound Calvinist, is "yoked to an unbeliever," Helen Jeffrey, an Episcopalian who is so devoted to her husband that she can ignore his bigotry if only he will permit her to. He believes, however, that the salvation of her soul is more imperative than the survival of his home, sends her away, breaks down under the strain, and dies. Subplots are worth mention only because they are developed with the aid of a fatal runaway accident, a fatal mill fire, and a knockdown and drag-out fight. Mrs. Deland accepted her young bigot on his own terms; but her reading public could have accepted him only in the heresy-hunting mood that marked the time, and in the light of the interest reflected from Mrs. Humphry Ward's *Robert Elsmere*, which was an English ecclesiastical tale of quite a different color.

After 1868, which happens to be the year of both *Oldtown Folks* and *The Gates Ajar*, the dominant Congregational Calvinism, which is most often associated with Puritanism, went into a decline. The proliferations of denominationalism sapped its strength; and the Unitarians and Anglicans enlisted many of the alert and the élite. As a result the novels dealing with religion and the church led in two directions: either to apostasy from Puritanism or to a semi-satirical exposition of its decadent survivals. On the one hand were such books of the 1910 decade as Mrs. Deland's *The Iron Woman* and Winston Churchill's big best-seller *The Inside of the Cup*, and on the other such novels of the 1930's as Santayana's *The Last Puritan* and Marquand's pair: *The Late George Apley* and *Wickford Point*.

Just how definitely Mrs. Deland had moved along with her time appears in the contrast offered both to *John Ward* and *Oldtown Folks* by *The Iron Woman*, who belonged to the next generation. For with the turn of the century the popular mind changed from theory to action and from religion to practical ethics. *The Iron Woman* is a mature story, skilfully told. It contains melodramatic episodes, but they are organic, not superimposed. Mrs. Maitland, who

played the title role, and I use the past tense because
the book is so evidently dated, was at the outset of
the story a conventionally godly woman, as relent-
less in her Sabbath observance as she was in her
driving energy as a foundry manager; divided in
enthusiasm for the churches and for the factories
which were the chief assets of her industrial town.
As the story advanced, the old Puritan trio of thrift,
competence, and godliness were reduced to the first
two, and piling up money for her son became her
master-passion. The white spires which dominated
Oldtown and had once glorified Mercer were over-
topped and smoke begrimed by the belching foundry
chimneys; and while this was happening Puritanism
was not rejected for its narrowness; it was simply
discarded for its insufficiency in a machine age. " 'I
call that ladle,' said Mrs. Maitland standing in her
foundry, 'the cradle of civilization. Think what's
inside of it. There are rails . . . . and engines and
machines for the whole world; there are telegraph
wires. There are bridges in it, and pens that may
write . . . . love letters, or even write, perhaps, the
liberty of a race, as Lincoln's pen wrote it. Yes,'
she said, her face full of luminous abstractions, 'the
cradle of civilization.' "

It might be objected to Churchill's *The Inside of
the Cup*, which appeared soon after *The Iron Woman*,
that it should not appear in this context, as it is a

story of the Middle West. But the middle-western city, obviously St. Louis, in which it was located, was an offspring of New England, intellectually dominated in 1868, the first year mentioned in the story, by Eliots and Hosmers, Larneds, Carpenters, and Greenes, Unitarian apostates from Calvinism; and the leading character, Rev. John Hodder, was brought there from a Vermont parish, a Calvinist of Calvinists, garbed in the vestments of an Episcopal rector.

In 1912, when the story appeared in serial form, the hunt for heretics was apparently a thing of the past, and the so-called Fundamentalist movement was still to come. The religious swing of the moment was from faith to works, from a concern with individual salvation to programs for social service. Theology was yielding the stage to New Testament exegesis, so that the layman could read disquisitions and the student elect courses on the social teachings of Jesus. Even in this field the foreign missionary was becoming more and more occupied with hygiene and sanitation, and the church "benevolent funds" recognized more and more liberally that charity began at home. The metropolitan church added a social center to the plant, and visiting nurses and recreational directors to the staff. All this demanded something new of the minister—that he be a practical administrator, a good money-raiser, and an effective citizen. But the practical money-raiser and the model of good citizenship was bound, if he retained any sense of the kingdom of heaven, to face two grim facts: that much of the money that came from the rich was only partial restoration of ill-gotten gains; and that the social center was only an offer of palliatives and correctives for the abuses of an un-Christian economic system.

The Inside of the Cup gave, in the experience of the Reverend John Hodder, a recapitulation of this chapter in social history. Brought from Vermont to a city pulpit in one of the many western outposts of New England, he was chosen for the post because he gave every sign of having sound views. The corporation lawyer who selected him was satisfied; the captain of finance who dominated the parish as he dominated every organization he belonged to was highly pleased. All went smoothly for six months. The sermons were excellently uplifting and undisturbing; plans for the new community house expanded grandiosely. Then he was waked up to the insufficiency of offering reading-rooms and gymnasiums to the poor, and to the inconsistency of preaching the brotherhood of man to a parish which opposed it even while paying him his salary. With his attempt to apply Christian principle to doing God's will in St John's downtown parish in the

slum district, Mr. Hodder, now enlisted in the
church militant, "went over the top." Events
moved fast. The rector won the admiring indorsement of his bishop, the strong minority of his con-
gregation, a large accession of followers, and, for
the story's sake, the daughter of the big financier,
Eldon Parr. The magnate was left humiliated and
deserted by his child; and the book closed with a
declaration of war, which on moral grounds could
end only with defeat for Dives and victory for the
forces of righteousness. Actually it was the Puritan
quality of John Hodder, moral crusader, which
dominated the situation. But it was only when he
was brought into the world of action from the theological fastnesses of the Vermont hills that he
found himself. Mr. Hodder is like Mrs. Stowe's Dr.
Hopkins of *The Minister's Wooing* in opposing Christian doctrine to the business interests of his richest
parishioner; but he differs in transferring his zest for
doctrines as doctrines to a zest for establishing Christian doctrines as guides for social conduct.

Two points are obvious as to all these novels
about churchmen and the church: that the authors
were parts of their subjects, most of them period
writers going along with the times of which they
wrote; and that the popularity of the novels arose
from the fact that the readers also were bystanders in

the novels and therefore responsive to them. American religious life had had to tune itself to American secular life until at last the roar of the factory whistle and the hubbub of the stock exchange had drowned out choir and organ, and the worship of Mammon prevailed.

The facts surrounding Santayana's *The Last Puritan* are quite different. The reading public was still in sympathy with the author, but neither reader nor author was in sympathy with the central figure in the story. Oliver Alden is presented as a relic of an old order, a character with an obsolete theory of life; and he is confronted not by liberal theology or heresy or worship of the golden calf but by a twentieth-century secular philosophy. This was an attitude toward life which the theologians of Dr. Hopkins' day sneered at as "philosophism" and in darker moods berated as infidelity, atheism, diabolism, that let loose the natural depravity of the natural man and dragged him into a sink of wickedness on his way to hell. Furthermore, the novel was written by a departed sojourner in New England, a philosopher, observer, and critic, a Spaniard by birth and a Roman Catholic by profession. None of these other writers could for a moment rival George Santayana in acuteness of intellect, power of analysis, philosophic expertness, and skill in dialectic. The fact that they were participants in the action which they described limited them in powers of detachment. The distinction is important that the picture of the "last puritan" was painted by a visiting artist who had tarried in New England long enough to write intimately and expertly, who was not at all hostile to his subject, but who was also not in the least in sympathy with it.

Mr. Santayana uses the word Puritanism in a clear but quite untechnical sense to mean a form of cultural tradition not necessarily local, but once dominant in New England and now on its final decline there. He defines it at no one point, but he characterizes it often. Puritanism, in his view, is a natural reaction against nature; in order to escape chaos it is ready both to impose, and to submit to, the sternest regimen. It abjures happiness and seeks peace even under the crunching of a moral juggernaut. It discards the fleshly life, it rejects the life of refinement, "merry without claims, brave without armour"; and it elects to be "burdened but strong, groping but faithful, desolate but proud." It insists on being self-directed, inflexible but free. It can reluctantly tolerate men and women of other minds, but it cannot sympathize with them; and for the sake of its own salvation it can turn its back in self-imposed exile upon the world, the flesh, and the devil.

Oliver Alden, who embodies all this, is the immediate reflection of two discordant elders, his father and his uncle. Uncle Nathaniel was a solitary, the custodian of a great fortune, an extreme survival with a brave loyalty to his breeding, who would not permit the world to override him and who kept himself inviolate by holding himself aloof. Oliver's father, Peter Alden, was a living protest against this; he opposed the conventions, denied social responsibility, was indifferent to moral reputation or business repute, became an aimless cosmopolitan globe-trotter, and when his life wearied him he brought it to a decent conclusion with the aid of a judiciously compounded sleeping potion. He paused once in his wanderings long enough to marry a smug, healthy New Englander, and after Oliver had reached his teens he was interested to see that his son should grow up in such freedom as he might achieve for himself.

Herein lay the conflict. Oliver was not allured by pleasures and palaces, but when he looked for an equivalent he could find no sweet home for his spirit. In his natural reaction against nature he was drawn to Lord Jim, skipper of his father's seagoing yacht, but repelled as by a fine beast of the jungle; he was dazzled and amused by his worldly cousin Mario Van Der Weyer, but only as he might be by a youth who was as promiscuous as an English sparrow and unstable as a butterfly. He considered mar-

riage to a conventional New Yorker who coquetted
with art, social ideals, and religion, until he found
that she was proposing to annex him and adapt him
to her life. Distrusting himself, he "kept revising
himself." He was afraid of the nature of love, always disturbed by the fear of desire. He was burdened by wealth, the chance that had thrown it into
his hands, the question of what to do with it. Even
his fine physical endowments were a source of more
embarrassment than pride. So to the end of his short
life during the World War, an innate cautiousness,
an all-pervading thrift, made him in every sense an
example of what in one special sense we have come
to describe as "poverty in the midst of abundance."

So much for the world of circumstance. There
was no happier solution for him in the world of
ideas. "He could find no peace unless he justified his
natural sympathies theoretically and turned them
into moral maxims." Secular philosophy did not do
him this service; and when, in the other direction,
he inquired of Roman Catholicism, he was too
earth-bound and too literally occidental in his habits of mind to rest his case at the same time on belief
in the human heart and belief in the supernatural, to
depend up to a certain point on unaided intellect
and, beyond that point, "to appeal to the higher
court."

Although this was Santayana's sole excursion

into the realm of the novel he was acute enough not to venture where he could not safely tread. A few paragraphs in the epilogue laid down quite clearly certain principles of narrative technique. Projecting his characters through the medium of his own mind, expressing their thoughts frankly in his own idiom, he nevertheless created real characters, dialogue, episodes. Oliver Alden was a chill young man, but there was a pathos in his chillness which came from a lack of spiritual warmth though from no lack of inward friction. Withal, the novelist concluded, "fortune will never smile on those who disown the living force of nature"; and Oliver, the last Puritan, illustrated the tragedy of his kind because "he was endowed with a moral nature burdened and over-strong, and a critical faculty fearless, but helplessly subjective." Oliver was heroic enough to afford the makings of tragedy. His uncle Nathaniel and his father Peter both lived so apart as to wither early into amiable ghosts. Such characters offer material for light satire, an offer happily accepted by John P. Marquand.

In his account of the amiable ghost, George Apley, Mr. Marquand seems to have made explicit acknowledgment to Mr. Santayana and Nathaniel Alden. The earlier book was subtitled "A Memoir in the Form of a Novel." The later, "A Novel in the

Form of a Memoir," serves as the neatest of parodies on a literary form which flourishes in Bostonia.
George Apley would have been highly approved by
Uncle Nathaniel; his wife and sister would have
been quite at home with Oliver's mother. Both the
men were pew-holders in Unitarian King's Chapel,
offshoots in creed but offsprings in character from
the Puritanism of an elder day. The parallel, however, could easily be pursued too far. *The Last Puritan* is an analytical study; *The Late George Apley* is a
genial caricature.

Apley's forebears came to Boston in 1636, and
from then on the Apleys looked down their noses at
the commoners of Plymouth. In the direct line one
was mentioned by Cotton Mather in his *Magnalia*,
and every generation had its representative at Harvard. All married discreetly, though one met the
family disapproval by stooping to an alliance with
a Cabot. Conservative by nature and industrious in
amassing property, they shrank from the disturbing
influences of the Revolutionary and Civil wars. The
family fortunes were founded in commerce, reinforced in textiles, multiplied by judicious invest-
ment, guarded with thrift, and partially distributed
in dignified gifts to art and charity. Republicans
since the days of Lincoln, they shrank from everything that smacked of the republicanism of Jefferson. They believed in the quiet and practical exer-

tion of such influence as wealth could wield in a democracy.

Product of such a tradition, George Apley once explained, "I am the sort of man I am, because environment prevented my being anything else," environment in his mind being crystallized tradition. His world was a segment of a circle radiating about forty miles from Boston. Complacent at times, at other times he was merely submissive to the dictates of tribal loyalty. He lived within the pale of his family for whose reputation and fortune he was trustee, of his duties as distributor of largesse which his fortune demanded, and of the various clubs by which his inviolable respectability was buttressed. But he sacrificed his one real love on the shrine of family dignity, and to keep this dignity unsullied he used the family gold to buy his way out of a blackmail trap into which in a burst of misdirected civic zeal he had naïvely blundered. I have referred to the portrait as a genial caricature, but the term demands cautious use. George Apley was a type for social comedy but not a comic type. Emerson had him in mind when one day he confided to his *Journal* that *In Memoriam* sounded to him "like the condolences of prosperous Unitarians in the first weeks of bereavement," and when on another he wrote that the greatest obstacle to progress was "the invincible depravity of the virtuous classes." The comedy of this gentleman of the old school was that he always concealed from others, and usually from himself, that he was a frustrated man; the pathos was that he now and again perceived this fact, acknowledging in his inmost heart that there was little to justify his outward complacency.

In this respect George Apley was a man of a higher level than the Brills of *Wickford Point*, the most ghostly of decadent Puritans, who had nothing to be proud of but their self-esteem and who were far from amiable even in their esteem for one another. Again we may consider the novelist's point of view. Mr. Marquand's is midway between that of Mrs. Stowe, who was completely identified with the Puritan tradition, and that of Mr. Santayana, who was completely detached from it. The author of *Wickford Point* feels more affection for the Puritan gone to seed than he does for the ex-Puritan-Brahmin of the Apley type. The Brills have interbred until they have nothing left but pride of family—neither money nor brains nor resolution nor high moral sense. They embody "an inexorable sort of gentleness, a vanity of effort, a sadness of predestined failure." They are haunted by the ghost of a vanished security. Wickford Point is an island adrift, once part of the mainland, self-sufficient though severed from reality, and "governed by the untutored thoughts of women." It is a world built up to keep out the real world and intrenched in futility.

Wickford Point is interesting for many reasons which are not relevant in this chapter: its structure like a braided Indian basket, spiraling from bottom to rim, firmly interwoven, but dizzying to follow; its characterization, which supplies us with more than a dozen convincing portraits; its dry New England humor and use of understatement; its revelation of Mr. Marquand's pet antipathies; its running comment on literary American fashions. But it is introduced here only because it concludes the sequence of American novels which, taken as a whole, tell of New England Puritanism's fall from high estate. This is not in fact a complete or completed story; but it is the story as told by recent novelists, and it is significant because they composed it without collaboration and because the reading public has responded so largely to its successive instalments.

IV
Joseph Hergesheimer

IN *San Cristobal de la Habana*, which belongs in his early years of publication, Joseph Hergesheimer wrote at length of arriving one day in Havana, going to the hotel, dressing, and dining. For the average traveler, even the average traveler with more than average keenness of observation, the first hours in Havana would be filled with impressions of the differences between this place and other places, the look of the harbor, the docks, the streets, the hotel lobby, the people, and their costumes and manners. But "each man's life shall have its proper lights," and this particular traveler postponed the record of these broader aspects of the picture. For the moment he had to adjust himself to new and near surroundings and to prepare himself for a ritual. So at the outset his eyes were chiefly for his room. He liked its high coolness and the splashes of light that slanted across the wall through a varicolored lunette. His spirit could repose here. So he laid out his clothes, bathed, and dressed, with special attention to the texture and tone of his necktie, experimenting gravely until he was satisfied. He descended to the dining-room, secured the proper table for the enjoyment of proper food and drink, and proceeded to the meal itself, a sequence of delectations for an unjaded palate. After it, in the soft evening air, with the lighting of the proper cigar, he sent up fragrant incense to the minor but important god of gustation.

To the man who had written *Linda Condon*, and who was to write *The Bright Shawl* and *The Party Dress*, life had become in all its hours a refinement of sensuous experiences. Food was only incidentally sustenance. Clothes should be pleasant to see and touch. And a house was less than nothing when conceived of only as a shelter. It should be an expression of the complete man, a resort in which his soul expands, an asylum of the spirit. For this American, used to the amplitudes and the amenities from childhood, a house must be incarnate age and rockbound stability. In the perpetuation of the past it must give foothold for criticism of the present. It must be so solid that it receives only on sufferance the resident of the moment. And it must be exacting in its demands on him, reaching out through him and securing from their hiding-places in the past the chairs and tables and chests and rugs and pewter and glass that inevitably belong in it. It must be the work of art that life itself should be, surrounded by turf and tree that perennially renew the past and

beautify the passing moment. It should motivate
the art of the writer in it, so that he writes to support it, gathers data in its interest, brings his rewards to its hearthstone as to an exacting mistress,
and finds that for his farther reward "it upholds him
with an inviolable whispered calm."

Such a house prolongs for him the quiet of an
early Quaker pastoral in the midst of a tumultuous
present. It promotes the spirit of the patriot, as that
spirit roots itself in the love of land and fireside,
depresses him with a sense of social disintegration
around him, and reawakens in him the faith of the
federalist, who is nearest to the traditions that prevailed when the house was builded and who is most
skeptical about the democratic experiment that
would in time substitute prefabricated bungalows
for homesteads that stand foursquare against the
winds of innovation.

So Hergesheimer installed himself in such a homestead (and he told all about it in the pages entitled
From an Old House, though oddly enough they were
written not from under its rooftree but from a
rented room in town), and, once installed there, he
weighed past and present in the balance. He was a
Presbyterian child of a rich, aristocratic past, the
kind of past to which Linda Condon, born of the
Lowries, returned when she became Linda Hallet.

What he cherished from this past was not the religious belief but the capacity for enjoyment and an admiration for the independence of mind and action that belongs to the well-intrenched aristocrat. He missed just those traits in the present. He knew quite well that his father and grandfather would look askance at his writings; that his grandfather would detest *Cytherea*, regard *Linda* as a mad performance, and pass *The Lay Anthony* without a word; that he would approve the backgrounds of *The Three Black Pennys*, *Java Head*, and *Balisand;* and that he would fully understand *Mountain Blood* because it was so completely Presbyterian.

The judgment of the past would afford him no great honors; and he felt slight respect for the judgment of the present, though fortunately, after long withholding, it was lavish enough to afford him escape from the intolerable and to supply him the privacy and freedom to put into words the thoughts that intrigued him. This response of the public was the more fortunate because he did not subscribe to their romantic formula and did not intentionally compound with them. He did not see many heroes about him and tried to write of men who did not perform prodigies of valor or achieve the reward of happy endings; and the women he wrote of did not please the women, because as an old Tory he preferred his women to be rather more charming than efficient, which seemed belittling to the contemporary feminist. However, he went on his way, a little amused and a good deal surprised that he had cleft the rock of prejudice with his pen and that a rivulet of gold was flowing therefrom.

In a passage of self-analysis, Mr. Hergesheimer made himself imperatively quotable on the subject of his characters: "I didn't particularly, the truth was, admire my own character; I should not— except for the ability of work—have chosen it. I liked calmness and I wasn't calm; I liked fidelity, and except to my writing, I wasn't conspicuous for it; I liked hardness of body, a condition I hadn't the perseverance to keep; I liked, for myself, in vain, a distinguished resolution in bearing and mind." Lacking these characteristics, he said, he thought them uncommonly desirable, and he made them live on paper. But he omitted from this list another trait which he has had—a sense of formality coupled with independence of mind and conduct. These are the heritage of the nonconformist aristocrat. It belongs to all the black Pennys, but no less to Isabel Penny, supercultivated but resiliant as Damascus steel. It belongs to Linda Hallet who, like Isabel, could with unraised pulse defy her husband in behalf of palpitant youth. It is a part of Richard Bale who, on the morning of a duel to the death, can tell his wife only by indirection of the sentiment, too deep for words, which possesses him for home and homestead. It is a part, and the dominant part, of Tao Yuen, who comes to America from a civilization measured by millenniums and whose implicit but unmistakable vitality is never betrayed into outward expression. These men and women are the natural creations of an author who could say for himself, "Complete formality, it seemed to me, provided a mask behind which the individual could rest, retire, unwearied by the endless fatigue of personal contacts."

Surrounded by complete formality in his housing, and controlled by the part of himself which was his home, he resolved after early wanderings of the imagination never again in his writings to depart from the traditions of America, to stray from the mood of Dower House. It is a mood not dissimilar from that of *The House of the Seven Gables*, which can be re-created from the past of all the seaboard towns from Salem to New Orleans. Yet he did not do this with the resolution of the historical novelist. He rather chose, or acknowledged, the idiom in which he must write, and was concerned with the facts only as they were expressive of the mood. His intent was to connect "a bygone time with the very present that is flitting away from us," prolonging a legend, to continue with Hawthorne's words, "from an epoch now gray in the distance, down into

our own broad sunlight and bringing along with it
some of its legendary mist." As the mood is timeless and the idiom only that of thought and action,
Hergesheimer, like Hawthorne, spoke in the language of his own day, abjuring the archaisms of the
past. And he expressed the perennial idioms of life
partly in capacities to enjoy the best of life's sights
and sounds and partly in larger capacities for
strength and constancy and courage.

Like Hawthorne, again, he seldom forgot that
"the very present is flitting away from us." It is an
inevitable feeling for characters whose eyes are fo-
cused on the past. A minor key prevails throughout
his pages: the key sounded on the entrance of Jasper
Penny, "conscious of the invidious beginning
weariness of accumulating years," and on the entrance of Richard Bale, just past thirty but weary of
the strife of years, aware that life has but the frail
duration of a flower, and that the most fleeting
quality of a flower is its fragrance. To Jasper and to
Richard renewal of youth is offered and mockingly
withheld. The hand of the past is on them as the
present slips away.

Richard Bale would have felt at home in Dower
House. He had fought under Washington, he was a
good Federalist, he belonged to the soil, and he
loved his country because he loved to feel it under
his feet. He fell in love with the betrothed of his

host, but delayed action only long enough to tell of his love and venture his life for it. After her death he could cherish his heart's desire to the end of his days and yet be true to his duties as husband, father, lord of a manor. He could live as a man who loved honor and embodied courage and was all unaware of possessing any fine and lofty sentiments; and withal he could drink and gamble and lose his temper and quarrel superbly. He could fulfil a formula which his literary creator would have liked to fulfil, of maintaining courage in the face of disaster, and he could do it in a chronicle that came to no happy ending, but to an ending that was not unheroic.

Richard Bale, committed to a cause, had to follow it at any cost. Worn with the struggle of the Revolutionary War, he had progressed from a devotion to Virginia, through a devotion to Washington, to a passionate attachment for the doomed cause of the privileged classes. A lower order of men were gaining control over a land to which they had been indifferent or renegade while the fighting was on. Even in retreat he was arrogant and obstinately insufferable to them. In love and politics he encountered a rival who seemed despicable to him. As they went down to death together, the old order passed.

The appropriate style for Richard Bale and his neighbors is more sumptuous than austere, and a natural one for a writer who studied painting before he took to the pen and who shows a feeling for surfaces and colors in everything he describes. There is a sensuous definiteness in the settings that one recalls in definite contours and lights and colors; and the historical details give the effect not so much of being carefully reconstructed as of being clearly recalled. Whether in description or in exposition Hergesheimer is able "to reproduce in the reader the emotion he would have felt under the same conditions."

Successful with the quieter scenes and the subtler situations, he is markedly successful with the more stirring episodes. No one who has read of it can forget the death of Lavinia Roderick, for he has realized it with something of the "searing completeness" that Richard had felt at the moment. No less vivid are the duel of Richard and Gawain Todd, and Gordon Mackimmon's defiance of the mob, and Honora Canderay's lashing of the scandalmonger, and the incomparable fencing episode in *The Bright Shawl*, and a dozen other passages. They are vivid scenes because they were vividly felt by people of keen perceptions and quick responsiveness. They could not have been the same to actors who did not know the finer enjoyments and the speechless dignities.

But *Balisand* was the last novel of which these things could be recorded. Mr. Hergesheimer was overtaken by the present—had already been so over-taken when in *Balisand* he once more reverted to a period gray in the distance. Before the change came, however, one had come to accept the master of Dower House on his own terms. One thought of him as most at home with the people of his imaginings. There was a clank of the knocker, and he stood in the hall to greet his guests as the butler opened to them. In came Richard Bale and Lavinia and the sturdy-hearted Lucia, and the three far-separated generations of the Pennys, and Linda Hallet and Arnaud, her husband, and John Woolfolk—all conscious of their forebears but all aware of Tao Yuen the imperturbable, the only one in whose veins flowed four thousand years of cultural heritage. One could guess at slight surprises and the beginnings of questions that were not uttered. At table the talk was of the past, and on the common ground of old tradition there were mellowing responses of word and glance. Finally before the board was cleared and the ladies withdrew there was an instinctive turning toward the lord of the manor. He rose and looked about him with the friendly confidence of a youthful patriarch. It was a May evening, and through the open windows the strains of dance music came down from the neighboring clubhouse. The room was aglow with the shaded candlelight which did not quite outshine the twilight of a day that was past. And as his guests turned to him he addressed them in words which for the time and place were altogether fitting and proper: "Ladies and gentlemen," he said.

Lee Random and Savina Grove would not have been at home in this company. As *Cytherea* testifies, Mr. Hergesheimer had not been able to resist the assault of modernity upon the home of his imagination and he was headed toward an almost total surrender. He had become self-conscious in behalf of Dower House, aware that it was a conspicuous survival from the past. More than that, that it was in fact a restored antique with modern plumbing and electric lights. Below the terrace and the formal garden was a putting green, from which it followed that, on a knoll near the first tee and sheltering the "nineteenth hole," a locker-room well stocked with liquor, was a country clubhouse. Mr. Hergesheimer tells of an evening when sitting on his terrace alone he heard the music for a party drifting down to him. It was for the casual dancing of the present, millenniums later than the generation of the minuet and immemorially later than that of even the polka and waltz and schottische. These latter rhythms were momentarily in the music only to give way to the mad fervors and hysterical moods appropriate to negroes at a *danzon*, "a confusion of

(63)

forms very like the age . . . . the assault of a persuasive discontent."

These phrases apply not only to the trend of his later books but also to a great body of fiction that was soon to be written; in his own output they apply most especially to *Cytherea*, *Tampico*, and *The Party Dress*. *Cytherea*, the book, for example, is a confusion of forms, just as Cytherea, the doll symbol, is the assault of a persuasive discontent. Lee Random, central character, is a completely modern businessman with no trace in his makeup of traditional distinction, calmness, fidelity, hardness of body, or resolution. Compounded of the opposites and a kind of lazily accidental business acumen, he lives in a business world, in a piece of modern domestic architecture, on the edge of a golf course, with a wife whom he persists in regarding as a model, although as the story presents her she is a plaintive nagger and a potential termagant as events rapidly prove. Lee is ready for Cytherea, symbol of alluring womanhood, and for Mrs. Grove, temporary fulfilment of the Cytherean longing. In her he encounters a woman who is supreme "on the plane of absolute civilization." She inflames him not as a potential mother but as a completely seductive being. What now stirred him, said the author, had nothing to do with breeding. It shortly turns out that it also had nothing to do with good breeding.

For the course of Lee and Savina is the course of the clubhouse vulgarians, impossible for the gentlefolk of *Java Head* or *Balisand*. It starts with a gross violation of hospitality, slips off into a furtive elopement, and culminates in a fatal orgy of sexual excess. Such things have happened, but not to the people with whom Mr. Hergesheimer first consorted in his books.

When in *Cytherea* he abandoned the code of Dower House for the code of the golf club, he found in the rhythms of the dance music, even as he was mounting the hillside, that both roofs sheltered one thing in common. For the assault of a persuasive discontent is the genesis of romantic feeling in all times and all climes. That is what stirred the mountain blood of Gordon Mackimmon, quickened the slow pulse of the pallid aristocrat, Honora Canderay, and drove Dodge Playdon, sculptor, and Alexander Hulings, ironmaster, each to his achievement. In this tale Hergesheimer set the hectic and meaningless pursuit of pleasure over against the dream of the unattainable. It is the approach of Mr. Cabell in the run of his stories—in *The Cream of the Jest* most obviously. Felix Kennaston, to reach his end, seeks romance by a flight from Litchfield to Storisende, but nightly finds something in Storisende to reconcile him to Litchfield. The unattainable is in truth unattainable; the near approach to any object of desire dissolves the dream and recalls the present but casts over the present something of the aura of the dream. The clarity of the story is comparable to the formula for the square of $x + y$, which is $x^2 + 2xy + y^2$; the letters—let them stand as symbols for the near and the remote—overlapping though they are clearly separable.

It is something of this sort on which Hergesheimer ventured in *Cytherea*, and which in a virtual epilogue Lee Random struggled in vain to explicate to his astutely drowsy brother. The doll Cytherea had represented something unknown that he had vaguely desired. She was a doll, more fascinating than any woman, but she was a principle. In time she was translated into a very individual woman. Lee fell into the error, as he was speculating about the values in life, of putting himself and Savina Grove into the places of x and y. "I . . . . made the mistake of thinking that I, as an individual, had an importance. In my insane belief that a heavenly beauty, a celestial chorus girl, was kept for me, I pictured myself as an object of tender universal consideration." Finally, after the catastrophe, when his wife made a return possible, he had the acumen to see that he could not resume personal relationships with a social order that he had so personally defied. He had rationalized himself out of existence in a concrete world.

(66)

Joseph Hergesheimer

But the assault of a persuasive discontent was responsible for more than this; it not only made ducks and drakes out of Lee Random's life, it warped Joseph Hergesheimer out of his own orbit. "It hadn't the power to remove me from the terrace, and yet it was vaguely disconcerting." Probably because the assault was not overwhelming the novel was only relatively shapeless and indeterminate. Because of the marked unity of tone and atmosphere in the preceding novels, the first impression of this one is of extraordinary disorder. A second thought tempts one to conclude that the disorder was calculated. But a third thought compels one to admit that, though the conception is intrinsically sound, confusion was inherent in the tale, for lack of any such standards as the Pennys could be measured against. Fanny, the dull and faithful wife, to play her part in drama, should be impeccable and at least negatively admirable; but in conduct and speech she is neither as dull nor as desirable as Lee insists she is. Lee, to be a convincing sport of the gods, should come to a tragic ending. It is in a way tragic that he should resign himself to oblivion and speculate on whether drinking cannot serve him perennially distilled delusions. But no tragedy is complete that is unrecognized by the victim; and no story is tragic in execution that acknowledges by appended pages of exegesis its own failure to convey the point.

Cytherea carries an old-fashioned moral, and Mr. Hergesheimer half-heartedly attempted to explain it. It is what the clubhouse did to him with its disconcerting melodies and rhythms. *Cytherea* only emphasizes the charm of the works that were written in the mood of the old stone pile below the clubhouse.

In *The Party Dress*, eight years later, Hergesheimer came rather more firmly to grips with the confusion of the age, in another country club tale. The club vulgarians are not quite so vulgar; the victim of the age, a woman this time, is by no means as crass as her husband, who is the replica of Lee Random. Nina Henry half comprehends what is going on in social history. She sees that her seventeen-year-old daughter is not merely perverse but that she reflects the "doubts and questions of a doubtful time" and that the underlying trouble was that "almost no one now believed in much." In rebellion against what could not be changed or helped she degrades herself and her lover, and reaps the tragic result of his suicide.

In his fine fervor for the traditions of Dower House, Mr. Hergesheimer once resolved never again to lapse from its mood in his writings; but, not conspicuous for fidelity, he ignored the resolution when he wrote *Tampico*, returning to the mood of the clubhouse and the humid sensuousness of Central

America. On the surface *Tampico* seems to fit the early Hergesheimer formula, but only on the surface and at first glance. It is in fact a sort of anticlimactic sequel to what the master of Dower House would have done with these same materials a dozen years earlier. Govett Bradier, at the opening of *Tampico*, had pursued a brilliant and remorselessly successful career as an oil prospector and operator in Mexico. He returned from New York to the scene of his achievements to take possession of the wife of an old friend. He found himself suspected of business dishonesty toward the man whose love he was despoiling. In the effort to clear up the charge of a particular type of infidelity of which he was innocent, faith unfaithful kept him falsely true for a while; but this flash of a fine old integrity was dimmed as he blundered along through malarial attacks, drinking excesses, bawdy-house episodes, and miscellaneous blood-lettings until he lost power, position, the friend, the wife, and slipped furtively away from the scene of his defeat with nothing accomplished of what he had come to do.

Tampico is a novel of disintegration; but it is also a document in literary history. All those earlier works of Mr. Hergesheimer, drawn from American history and written against an aristocratic tradition, seem vitally different from *Tampico*, partly because they are so similar. The central figures are men of power, measurably self-controlled but ungovernable by outer control. They behave and misbehave like gentlemen, dominated by a set of convictions about personal honor and sex chivalry and class loyalty which they are willing to die for. These convictions are rather primitive and not very noble, but they are nevertheless ennobling because they stimulate positive faith and positive action. Govett Bradier was a man of this type during his active life as an oil producer before the opening of *Tampico*.

But in this story it is not Bradier who dominates, but Hergesheimer. And Hergesheimer was being charioted away from recognition of the old-fashioned controls by two spirited horses. One of them, already cited, was the trend of the period; but this was in harness with another—the Cytherean mood of a northerner during his early experience with the tropics, something which began way back with *San Cristobal de la Habana*. It is a common phenomenon in literature. We need go no farther than Melville and Hearn for examples of the experience. It starts with a delighted acceptance of the sensuous opulence in earth, sky, and sea. It is followed by a sensuous relaxation of the usual controls. In the tropic zone the gentleman finds his manners less instinctive than he had thought them in a cooler clime, and as his linen loses its starch his convictions do likewise. Then, when these are lost there is nothing left of his well-bred self but occasional reminiscent gleams of gentility. His drunken boastings and his cheap profanity would disgust Richard Bale; and if Richard Bale would lift an eyebrow and shrug a shoulder at Govett Bradier, so would Howat Penny at the Hergesheimer who opened a magazine essay with the salute, "I am getting damned tired of art!" Maybe he was; maybe he ought to have been, of the pseudo-art he had in mind; but he expressed himself in a tropico-ultramodern style as none of the Pennys would have done.

Apparently after liberal indulgences in this mood it ceased longer to satisfy Mr. Hergesheimer himself. In his latest novel, and perhaps his last, for *The Foolscap Rose* appeared in 1934, Wigton Kinzer says to his Victorian mother, "I'll admit something to you, and it is this, I worship the way you are. Stay like that, lovely and serene, and be sorry for us who have to be different. It can't be helped. You can't stop it." Not being able to resist the present effectively or to share it in "a distinguished resolution," Hergesheimer returned to the American past—the history in *Swords and Roses* (1929), the biography of *Sheridan, a Military Narrative* (1931), and two final romances, *The Limestone Tree* (1931), a Kentucky chronicle extending from the French and Indian

War till after the Civil War, and *The Foolscap Rose*
(1934), a Pennsylvania chronicle reaching from the
presidency of Andrew Jackson to that of Theodore
Roosevelt. There are the same technical excellences
in these later romances that I have cited in the early
ones on which his first reputation was established—
a richness of texture, a vividness of episode, and a
reality of scenes and of characters within scenes.
But there is not enough consecutive interest in them
to carry the reader through the intricacies of genealogy and archeology. Character and episode are
submerged in history, and the tales become tales for
the antiquarian rather than romances for the reader
of prose narrative. As history they may be scrupulous, but as art they suffer from the subordination of
truth to fact. The successful Hergesheimer of *Java
Head* and *The Three Black Pennys* after being overwhelmed by the present has failed in his later efforts
to recapture the past.

V

James Branch Cabell

TWENTY-FIVE years ago Mr. Cabell held his place among American writers of fiction because he was the most aggressive and most discussed romantic novelist in the land. People who relished contrasts set him over against Theodore Dreiser. Dreiser believed in telling the whole truth about life, and he found factual truth on every hand revealed to the physical eye. Cabell contended that the only tolerable truth was the truth which repudiates the sordid and homely and wearisome facts. Dreiser's style was as homely as his material; Cabell's as ornate as his romantic dreamworld. Dreiser's life was identified with certain middle-western towns and cities; Cabell's with southern villages. Dreiser was a Puritan apostate—recalcitrant but still a Puritan in tradition; Cabell was a cavalier—a "peripatetic Episcopalian." They agreed at only one point—their dissent from the established conventional code—the rule of Mrs. Grundy. Dreiser ignored her or pushed her aside without apology, but Cabell was acutely aware of her presence and found a malicious pleasure in annoying her.

Knowing it would be useless to poison her soup, he took satisfaction in spoiling her appetite.

Because of their common contempt for the old lady they acquired much the same set of hostile critics; and the fierce assault on them both enlisted many of the same defenders. Dreiser was abused in his own brutal manner, and Cabell, who refrained from the use of short and ugly words, was bespattered with them. Few American authors have been so roundly berated: "slushy and disgusting," "worse than immoral—dull," "revolting," "a boudoir budget," "hardly excusable in print," "the whine of a little old man," culminating with the suppression of *Jurgen*. The violence of abuse rallied defenders of Cabell from those who had formerly been lukewarm about him.

The discussion of Cabell's ways and works has never been confined to his friends and foes, for he has always been his most prolific commentator. In the persons of certain story spokesmen, such as Manuel and Jurgen, Robert Townsend, Felix Kennaston, and John Charteris, he has stated his case in scores of passages and in dozens of ways. He has had no patience with the methods or the point of view of the realist: "No one on the preferable side of Bedlam wishes to be reminded of what we are in actuality, even were it possible, by any disastrous miracle, ever to dispel the mist which romance has evoked about all human doings." Says Charteris, "If ever I were to attempt a tale of Litchfield, I would not write a romance, but a tragedy. I think I would call my tragedy *Futility*, for it would mirror the life of Litchfield with unengaging candor; and, as a consequence, people would complain that my tragedy lacked sustained interest, and that its participants were inconsistent; that it had no ordered plot, no startling incidents, no high endeavors, and no special aim; and that it was equally deficient in all time-honored provocatives of either laughter or tears."

This fairly characterizes the stories of Litchfield which Mr. Cabell eventually wrote, notably *Cords of Vanity* and *The Rivet in Grandfather's Neck* (the remarks of Charteris come from the latter) though the author, instead of labeling them tragedies, sardonically called one "A Comedy of Shirking" and the other "A Comedy of Limitations." In *The Cream of the Jest*, Horvendile—one of Mr. Cabell's two disguises in this tale—takes up the theme: "There was once in a land very far away from this land—in my country—a writer of romances. And once he constructed a romance, which, after a hackneyed custom of my country, purported to be translated from an old manuscript. . . . . I am that writer of romance. This room, this castle, all the broad, rolling countryside without, is but a portion of my dream, and these places have no existence save in my fancies. . . . . I find my country an inadequate place in which to live. . . . . There is that in some of us which gets no exercise there; and we struggle blindly, with impotent yearning, to gain outlet for great powers which we know that we possess, even though we do not know their names. And so, we dreamers wander at adventure to Storisende—oh, and into more perilous realms sometimes!—in search of a life that will find employment for every faculty that we have.''

Storisende is in Cabell's Poictesme, ''which is bounded by Avalon and Phaeacia and sea-coast Bohemia, and the contiguous forests of Arden and Broceliande, and on the west of course by the Hesperides,'' a country which he believes ''to be the one possible setting for a really satisfactory novel, even though its byways can boast of little traffic nowadays.'' However, he does not confine his characters to even this imaginary realm. They wander in all directions—to Alexandria, Aquitaine, Arcadia, Asgard, to Barbary, England, Jerusalem, Massilia, to Navarre, Olympus, Portugal, and Rome. And they cover all chronology in their orbit around the thirteenth century from which most of their beautiful happenings are supposed to spring. ''Homer dreamed of you,'' says one of his lovers to one of his loved ones, "and Sophocles, and Theocritus. All poets have had glimpses of you." So he conjoins heroes and heroines in genealogies as inventive as his maps, and on a slender thread of heritage strings his garlands of slender stories, reaching through the ages, all dealing with the chivalric search for the unattainable, or with the gallant acceptance of the pleasures and inconveniences of life.

Mr. Cabell's avowed intention is to "write perfectly about beautiful happenings." For him this is not to achieve a perfect technique and then to exercise it with natural and spontaneous zest. It is to be a laborious pleasure-hunter. His style is like his use of geography and genealogy and his partly actual and partly invented authorities. It is like the painstaking play in words—the jest of the cream in *The Cream of the Jest*—which is wrought out concerning the sigil of Scoteia. Throughout the book this is described as a bit of metal which confers the magic power of invoking a dream life. At the end of the story it is explained as being a half of the broken top of a cold-cream jar marked with a design made up by "blending meaningless curlicues and dots and circles with an irresponsible hand." Yet in a blank page before the title there is a reproduction of the joined fragments; and the Cabell enthusiast whose

volume I read once ingeniously deciphered the
marks, which are upside down in the book, and
which declare that "James Branch Cabell made this
book, etc., etc." A deal of work for so obvious a
conclusion. One is by this time ready to be persuaded that the inscription thus deciphered is in itself a code, and that the quintessence of the cream is
yet to be extracted.

There is the same evidence of unstinted pains in
the prose style; and one deplores, of course, not the
pains but the evidence thereof. It is all wrought by
hard plodding, no step of which is easier for those
that have preceded. Cabell writes of proofreading:
"Here was the word vexatiously repeated within
three lines, which must be replaced by a synonym;
and the clause which, when transposed, made the
whole sentence gain in force and comeliness . . . .
and the vaguely unsatisfactory adjective, for which
a jet of inspiration suggested a substitute." Every
writer worth his salt revises in this fashion, but not
as follows, for: "Then you dip into an *Unabridged*,
and change every word that has been written for a
better one, and do it leisurely, rolling in the mouth,
as it were, the flavour of every possible synonym,
before decision. Then you read with a corrective
pen in hand the while, and you venture upon the
whole to agree with Mérimée that it is preferable to

write one's own books, since those of others are not, after all, particularly worth reading in comparison."

Such procedure does not lead to spontaneity of effect, and you do not find it in Mr. Cabell's pages. He anticipates criticism often and again, as in his own comments on Felix Kennaston, his (as he might put it) so obviously autobiographic character: "His high-pitched voice in talking, to begin with, was irritating; you knew it was not his natural voice, and found it so entirely senseless for him to speak thus. Then, too, the nervous and trivial grin with which he prefaced all his infrequent remarks . . . . was peculiarly uningratiating." Translated to prose style, these characteristics are Mr. Cabell's own on the printed page, justifiable only because their formality has some harmonious relation to the formalities appropriate to the doings in Poictesme. He adroitly overstates the indictment, and so tempts whoever quotes it to become an attorney for the defense by deprecating its severity even while indorsing its pertinence.

His romantic style is indubitably established, based on his conception of "urbanity," for which courtliness was perhaps the best equivalent in the days of chivalry. Yet it must be remembered that he has written sometimes as himself and very often in the manner of this, that, or the other author of whom he is evidently reminded. For himself he tends to long, but vertebrate, sentences, with interjected parentheses, inserted extra modifiers, inverted and transposed members. He is consciously suggestive of archaism without being too archaic; and he depends for relief effects through the introduction of marked and homely modernisms. On the whole the style is attractive; sometimes it is charming; but certain mannerisms, like those of Kennaston's speech, are monotonously affected. One wearies of the thousand-fold repetition of "a little by a little," "by ordinary," and of the preciosity of his pet adverbs like "kindlily" and "friendlily." It is just too pedantic to affix a second tail on an adjective that has an adverbial ending. And it is old-fashioned pedantry, too, to parade not only real but imaginary sources. This has been done from the Middle Ages to the age of Poe; and it has been done enough. The stories are overloaded also with historical preciosity. Aware that on the whole fancy is more important than fact to Mr. Cabell, the reader is distracted and annoyed by circumstantial matters of chronology and genealogy which delay action and throw no light on motive. He might well have taken a leaf out of a book of Howard Pyle, with whom he was early associated, and have emulated his elder's lucid mastery of the Robin Hood legend.

James Branch Cabell

To come back to earth, Mr. Cabell is a complete Virginian, which alone is enough to account for his love of fine and stately tradition. He has reconstructed the past as the archeologists, more literally and convincingly, have reconstructed his college town of Williamsburg. Only South Carolina would presume to challenge Virginia's right to be considered the sum and substance of the South. Only Virginia has the effrontery to take itself as seriously as South Carolina does; and the rest of the world takes it a little more so. They are both reminiscent states, as in varying degrees all the seaboard original colonies are. And the reminiscent quality of the South is of two quite distinct and highly contrastable kinds: its romantic chivalry turns back to a remote and idealized past; but its own gallant self reverts to a much nearer, quite disillusionized and sophisticated, eighteenth century—two sources which are worthy of more than a moment's consideration.

The remote past, and the idealized life found there, is the genuine Age of Chivalry, dominated by "a world-wide code in consonance with which all estimable people lived and died. Its root was the assumption (uncontested then) that a gentleman will always serve his God, his honor, and his lady without any reservation." It was a code under which gentlemen and ladies regarded themselves as children of an indulgent Father who was certain to deal out justice tempered with mercy; a code which later centuries outgrew after it had served society for many generations. It is the code which prevails in *Domnei*, a beautiful story of sublimated love; and to it in certain hours of disaffection with the modern "tragi-comic mêlée" the romantically disposed modern mind reverts with almost religious devotion. But such a reversion is possible only for those who can make it at a single, bold stride. The seeker for romantic relief must strip himself of every vestige of new-worldliness, and lend himself without reserve to the "willing suspense of disbelief" which stands between him and the chivalric code. This done, such a book as *Domnei* becomes readable and credible—a fine fruit of southern romantic faith. To fall short of this will result in a taste for *A Connecticut Yankee at King Arthur's Court*—a natural product of northern romantic skepticism.

If, however, one lack seven-century boots and if one be conscious of the long road back to medievalism, he falls on evil times, even in Virginia; for on the way he must pass through the eighteenth century, which is the parent of southern gallantry. What such a parentage means with respect to the romantic inheritance is revealed if we recall that the satirical *Rape of the Lock* was one of the earliest expressions of romantic unorthodoxy in the century of Pope and Johnson and that the ironic *Sense and*

Sensibility was a posthumous message. Whatever the contributory origins of southern speech and manners may be, they still resemble in some measure those that we associate with the days of Pope and Sterne and Jane Austen. Both behaviors are accompanied by a somewhat elevated formality of phrasing, an inclination to speak as from the rostrum, an opulent show of outward deference for beauty and womanhood, a vocal insistence upon honor and chivalry, and the stagey insincerity which follows hard upon the heels of conventionalized forms of speech. He who talks the language of gallantry today in America can do it in only two ways: with the smile of one who dances a minuet as a social accomplishment which no one takes seriously or with the covert contempt of one who is talking to intellectual inferiors. This gallantry is chivalry with its tongue in its cheek, and it is perfectly expressed in *Cords of Vanity: A Comedy of Shirking*. It is the South which is to be found, not quite so honestly, in lavender-scented reminiscenes of many other southern writers.

Mr. Cabell's approach to life is not so uncomplicated that it may be summed up in either woman worship, which is chivalry in perfection, as in *Domnei*, or in shirking, which is chivalry degenerate, as in *Cords of Vanity*. The greater part of his writing lies in the no-man's-land between. Of the stories of Poictesme, his ancient world, most are written with a covert smile if not, as in *Jurgen*, with a smirk. They are romances of two worlds, ostensibly about an ancient one though it is seen with modern eyes. Thus the "epistle dedicatory" to *The Line of Love* is addressed to Mrs. Grundy. This is minuet dancing at a fancy-dress ball—all very pretty, but only pseudo-romance. Of the stories of modern Virginia no other is so total a repudiation of chivalry as *Cords of Vanity*. In *The Rivet in Grandfather's Neck*, Rudolph Musgrave is a gentleman under the skin; but the code in this and others seems to be that a gentleman may ignore his God and need serve his honor and his lady only when convenient and agreeable.

One tale marks the balancing of the two worlds— *The Cream of the Jest*—in which Felix Kennaston, author, lives corporeally in a twentieth-century world, acquires two motors, money in four banks, an enlarged waistband, and a yearning for the romance which he finds nowhere about him. By means of his magic charm he is enabled to make off nightly to a world of dream and idyllic adventure. Everywhere, even in this world, he sees men and women scurrying through a jungle of confused circumstance "like feeble-minded ants," where he, and he only, can see the awe-inspiring design. Thrilled with a sense of beauty and order to which he is blinded in

Litchfield, he is buoyed through days of unimportant tasks and tedious, useless little habits. So, returning to daily life with the mocking sophistication of the school of gallantry, he yet carries back with him enough of the chivalric code to be true to his love—disavowing loyalty even while practicing it; to his Christian God, as proof of confidence in his creative artistry; and between the two, quite incidentally of course, to his own honor.

I have already quoted some of the harsh words directed at Mr. Cabell in the earlier part of his career. In rejoinder some of his more effusive friends, writing, by request, introductions to his subsequent works, were equally immoderate: "*Beyond Life* is on the threshold of its day as the *Sartor Resartus* of modernism." "In *Figures of Earth* he undertook the staggering and almost unsuspected task of rewriting humanity's sacred books." "The magnificent writing that is visible on every page." Yet there is no apparent need to consider him as either archfiend or demigod. The most admirable thing about him in his first monumental project was his persistence in writing his own kind of romance in his own way, until through ability and stupid hostility he achieved a wide hearing. He ought to be taken as seriously as he has taken, and still takes, himself, with a touch of tolerant skepticism. His prevailing mood has long been the youthful vanity

of Robert Townsend, who nevertheless was nobody's fool:

" 'That,' I airily said, 'is, in the first place, something you had no business to read; and, in the second, simply the blocking out of an entrancingly
beautiful poem. It represents a mood.'

" 'It is the sort of mood that isn't good for
people, especially for children. It very often gets
them shot full of large and very untidy holes.'

" 'Nonsense,' said I, but not in displeasure, because it made me feel like such a devil of a fellow.''

In 1929 with *The Way of Ecben* Mr. Cabell arrived
at the completion of what he calls the "Biography
of the Life of Manuel," describing it as a "book in
eighteen volumes." This book he relinquished to
James Branch Cabell as the finished project of that
author "in the exact form he designed and completed,—without any guess work as to his final
plans and with no blunders save his own, with no
inclusions untivitated by him, with no loose ends
anywhere, with no incongruous editing by other
hands, and (above all) with no lackwit replevinings
from his waste-paper basket conducted by his heirs
and creditors." Here stands the biography of
Manuel; there lies its author.

But the author has not been allowed to rest in
peace. Mr. Branch Cabell, his restless successor, has

seen to that in several volumes devoted to poking round among his ashes. Yet Mr. Branch Cabell, protest though he may, cannot escape the fact that he is the elderly relict of the young biographer, or that matter-of-factness has come along to clog the creative powers which subsided with his younger self, or that now the life of Manuel is done there is nothing left but to contemplate the life of James Branch Cabell.

In these later volumes, a handful of them, he repeatedly reverts to the former eighteen, tempting one to re-read and re-evaluate them with a temptation which is happily not irresistible. At some length he disavows ever having criticized or commemorated the "American Scene," mildly equivocating with the contention that the stories of Litchfield were not contemporary, were dated in the past, and failing to recognize that his device was a typically southern one; that up till the day before yesterday it was the established southern convention to make all local stories retrospective.

In a mock egoism which he acknowledges, he writes a trio of volumes related to his former self, the creator and lord of a vast imaginary domain. In the former eighteen volumes Poictesme was the setting for a series of romantic allegories. In these three volumes it is a dreamland. Smirt, Smith, and Smire are the ex-lords, and Lewis Carroll is the inspirer of the "Urbane Nightmare" which ensues there. It seemed, he explains, "increasingly necessary" that some one besides Lewis Carroll should develop a dream at length, and realistically, and with the imagination of an adult. This adult is a combination of the past Cabell and the extant one. He, or they, rather plume themselves on two or three points of dream psychology: their creatures have no sense of time, they do not move from place to place but surround themselves with whatever place they think of, and their sensory impressions are not fivefold, for they neither smell nor taste. "This sounds trivial enough," he asserts, and we agree. And hardly less trivial are the chief traits he attributes to Smirt-Smith-Smire. He is urbane, he is vainly recondite, he is a shadow of his own past, and he is incessantly priapic.

Herein lies the difference between a Carroll dream and a Cabell dream. The Alice books are "confined . . . . to the south temperate zone, as it were, in the callow, sexless dreams of a child," and the dreams are dreams that seem natural to all civilized people; the Smirt-Smith-Smire books offer adult dreams from the actual dreamer's point of view, reflecting his dreaming hours which belong to a highly eclectic, highly recondite, highly oversexed male. There is slight analogy between the callow dreams of Alice, which represent a common denominator in dreams, and the dreams of Smirt-Smith-Smire which are, to use Mr. Cabell's epithet, sex flavored and represent either a sex experience or a compensation sex desire which, I contend, is far from common. If anyone inquire how I can know this, my answer must be to quote Mr. Cabell on dreams: "It is my strong personal belief," and "These conditions are familiar to all mankind." Mr. Cabell's incessant ringing of the changes on cohabitation mark his failure to discriminate between a perennial obsession and the permanent principles for which he professes to feel an abiding concern.

This, however, is by the by. As in the earlier works, the elder Cabell in expounding himself has anticipated every criticism and has urbanely displayed his contempt for them all: He is a peripatetic Episcopalian dreaming that he is a bluebottle fly; he is at large pains to talk nonsense; he is looking back a bit wistfully on the high-pitched irrationality of his past; he traffics in farfetched and gaudy imaginings; and with ugly, illusive sniggerings; he is a tall chatterer whose tongue is in his cheek forever; his high dreams are offset by lewd appetites; his chief reward has been a cool, criticizing enjoyment. If these are hard words they are his words, for every one of which chapter and text can be cited; and, though they may have been uttered to excite polite protest, there is no reason for quarreling with them.

Beau Brummel has had his day and enjoyed it superbly, and, while having it, he has been picturesquely diverting, sometimes a little tiresome in his arrogant naughtiness, but usually amusing for his wit, and charming for the urbanity which he still cultivates with such youthful pride.

VI

The Retrospective South

SINCE 1920 or thereabouts no region in the
United States has talked and written so much
about itself as the South—the region from the
Ohio river to the Gulf and from central Texas to
Charleston, where "the Ashley and Cooper rivers
come together to form the Atlantic Ocean." Ser-
geant York, Muscle Shoals, the oil fields, Ben Till-
man and Tom Heflin, the boll weevil, Coca Cola,
Duke University, the Florida winter resorts, the
T.V.A., the negro migrations, Wendell Willkie,
Huey Long and the sharecroppers, soil erosion and
differential freight rates have all furnished matter
for researchers, journalists, novelists, and speculative social philosophers. Perusal of a fair share of
this output and of a dozen or more quite unscientific
trips to the South lead to certain conclusions: that
something is the matter, though there is no general
agreement as to cause or cure; that the malady is no
deeper seated in the South than corresponding ones
are elsewhere; and that the cure, if one be found,
will come from patient living and the human ad-
justments that take time rather than from inspired

schemes imposed by even the most benevolent Doers of Good or Economic Planners, endowed with the power to crack down on the sluggard and the obstructionist.

This region, it appears, is inhabited by whites and blacks—the blacks an inescapable factor in the situation because of the dependence of the whites on their labor, their dependence on the whites for support and direction, their own character, and their influence on the character of the race who were long ago their masters and who now sometimes love them, sometimes fear them, and often hate them. It appears that the white folk are classifiable in various ways. In time they belong to the old South, who refer to the War between the States and never forget it, the new South, who allude to the Civil War when and if they are reminded of it, and—in the nomenclature of a famous Boston church—the New Old South. Classified in social and economic terms, the whites in the South seem far more diversified than in other regions of the country. They include surviving planters in whom the old-time paternalism often survives; manufacturers, who sometimes combine violent antiunionism with the liveliest paternalism; the carriers and middlemen; the social theorists in college classrooms, newspaper offices, and, quite often, in governors' mansions; obviously, the white-collar class who are mentioned as seldom as they are elsewhere; the ranks of the employed of whom the South is actively and often painfully conscious: millworkers, fieldworkers, mineworkers, and shopworkers, convict laborers and then in a scale descending *ad infernum*, share-croppers, po' whites, and the increasingly mobile army of the unemployed. These all share one common possibility—invasion from the north by the institutional reformer, the labor organizer, the moral uplifter, or, a little less intolerably, by the millionaire and the tourist. And the South, according to one of its most candid selves, would rather be robbed than improved. It prefers "cruel perhaps but good-natured Southern carelessness" . . . . to the "ultimate malignancy of Yankee good intentions."

According to some southern commentators, and I draw only from spokesmen for the South, the troubles of the South are all due to the Civil War; but, according to others, they were coming to a focus before the war, which has ever since been used as a screen for southern deficiencies. Some say that ancestor worship and the lament for a golden age of doubtful authenticity form the screen. The worshipers reply manfully that a restoration of the elder culture would amount to a genuine renaissance. Some say, with more of history to verify them, that the conjunction of the two races was the tragic source of southern woes; some, that the invasion of northern commercial rapacity and corporate impersonalism is more of a nigger in the woodpile than the negro himself. Some ascribe conditions to agricultural improvidence and stupidity; others contend that the southerner never was born to be a farmer, that the trouble is in his distaste for the soil. Some blame it all on the sun.

For a while the southern Agrarians captured the center of the stage as champions of anti-industrialism and anti-Marxism. They assumed that "the responsibility of men is for their own welfare and that of their neighbours, not for the hypothetical welfare of some fabulous creature called society." They were for preserving in Dixie Land the best of an agrarian culture which was rapidly being overcome by northern industrialism. Explicitly, they were trying first of all to save the South from America; if by so doing America were also saved, they had no objection. And they were emphatically out of sympathy with those of their neighbors who hailed the new South, deplored the survival of outworn tradition, sang the praises of progress, and celebrated this progress with eloquent commentary and more eloquent statistics on looms and furnaces. They held a broad thesis against the ways of a capitalist society, which subsidized applied science, and against the consequent campaign for unlimited saving of labor, though to no defined end. They deplored overproduction, underemployment, multiplication of specious needs, haste to gratify them, and development of the conviction that "ideal living would consist of a series of good times unbroken by interludes of no place to go to."

They opposed to this industrialism an agrarian way of life, with the idyllic description of it as a life "in which agriculture is the leading vocation, whether for wealth, for pleasure, or for prestige—a form of labor that is pursued with intelligence and leisure, and that becomes the model to which other forms approach as well as they may." The definition suggested the popular and sardonic distinction between the agriculturist and the farmer, the acme of the system being obviously the agriculturist, living fully and richly in an old Kentucky home with its undeniable superiorities to a Park Avenue penthouse.

Quite naturally the Agrarians deprecated much in Thomas Wolfe, the southern apostate. Their representative, John Donald Wade, accused Wolfe of feeling no allegiance to his region and of caring for America only as a vague abstraction, a vast continent with trains roaring across it. He noted that Eugene's refrain was "Oh, lost!" and suggested that perhaps he could never be found until he was driven to a reconciliation with his origins. Even at that

Wade did not venture to claim him for a South of patrician origins or for the pursuit of agriculture. Wolfe replied (in *The Web and the Rock*) with amusement that he should be thought to lose strength, Anteus-like, by loss of contact with the soil and the atrophy of his root system. He found the Agrarians' concept of agriculture as vague as they found his nation concept, and derided them as "refined young gentlemen" who retired to the security of academic cloisters to distil their ideas in "precious magazines" which sang the praises of an agrarian society in quarterly instalments. "The subtler intelligence of this rebel hoard," he wrote, "were forever formulating codes and cults in their own precincts, codes and cults which affirmed the earthly virtues of both root and source in such unearthly language, by such processes of aesthetic subtlety, that even the cult adepts of the most precious city cliques were hard put to it to extract the meaning." More significant than this rejoinder is the comment of the ex parte observer Jonathan Daniels, who cannot escape the feeling that the Agrarians are already to be spoken of in the past tense or that there was a wide gulf between them and the actual South they were trying to save, so wide that he could establish no certain ground of understanding with the Agrarian whom he consulted at length. He contends that they have been too much derided, which is the damnation of faint praise. "But the dispersal of the Agrarians is complete." An examination of some typical fiction may explain why.

The cue to the temper of their symposium, *I'll Take My Stand*, is given in the title to the first essay "Reconstructed but Unregenerate," a reminder to the non-southerner that hot resentment can so long survive a war that has so few survivors. The cue to the central theme is supplied by Mr. Wade in a leisurely portrait sketch of "Cousin Lucius." Cousin Lucius, of slaveholding planter stock, born before the war, was sent to a Georgia Methodist college where he studied the classics, English literature, and southern eloquence in the first years of reconstruction. Hard times met him on his return. He could not beg; to labor on his father's farm he was ashamed; so he succeeded to the headship of a local academy, a gracious and benignant figure in a wide neighborhood, and the happy husband of Cousin Caroline, who had brought him, except for money, everything that a man might ask for in a wife. Yet, even when he inherited the paternal farm with its potential earnings, hard times still pursued.

Then, when he had reached middle age, someone found that Georgia had a new source of wealth in peaches and, by virtue of the refrigerator car, a new market in New York City. Before long Cousin Lucius was insidiously persuaded that "the master compromise had been achieved, that an agricultural community could fare well in a dance where the fiddles were all buzz-saws and the horns all steam-whistles." Advertising and salesmanship brought him a share in a swimming pool, a waning interest in the church, an enlarging acreage, the presidency of a local bank, universal respect, the decline of the peach industry, and the reimpoverishment of a countryside that had been taught in boom times to mortgage its insecure future along with its tangible possessions. This was what progress had done as the industrial North had given a lesson to the agrarian South. It is the lesson that the writers of this symposium took to heart and that is inherent in their creative writing. They attempted to make, in the words of Stark Young, "the most luminous defence" of their point of view by presenting "its noble embodiment in persons."

Stark Young, though an absentee landlord, seems to have established the most extensive literary estate among the agrarians. Others have discussed the principles of the school more insistently than he, but none has so popularly embodied the principles in a novel. But before coming to *So Red the Rose* it will be revealing to tarry a little at *Heaven Trees*, which preceded it by eight years. If Stark Young had not appeared as one of a school, and if the school had not claimed him as member, one might dismiss *Heaven Trees* as a frank echo of an echo—the early nineteenth-century revival of the early eighteenth-century Addisonian sketch. But as he is an acknowledged Agrarian, there is a point in this resemblance which is that a contemporary label has been affixed to something it does not describe. Joseph Addison was not interested in agriculture as a vocation, though he was interested in the country squire who depended upon it. Neither was Irving who carried the tradition of *The Spectator* over to *The Sketch Book*. Neither were A. B. Longstreet (whose biography has been written by John Donald Wade), nor John P. Kennedy. They too were concerned with transplanted country squires, now known as planters. Moreover, like Addison and Irving they were interested not in their planting but rather in their amiable eccentricities presented in "a rivulet of story wandering through a broad meadow of episode." "Or," said Kennedy, "a book of episodes with an occasional digression into the plot." Young, following these southern predecessors wrote of a social order in polite regret at its decline, offering a picture of the gentry, for the gentry, by one of the gentry, realistic only as it divested them of some of their courtly trappings and presented them as simple, fallible, moderately uncultured, rural gentlemen. Very naturally and appropriately *Heaven Trees* has the structure and style

of the Addison-Kennedy tradition. But there is one
fundamental difference. Young belongs to the twentieth century which no longer insists upon a moral-
istic interpretation and justification of life. These
earlier southerners shared the assumptions of their
generation and not only rang the changes on the
moral implications of every tale, incident, speech,
and action, but were also extremely chary of shocking the sensibilities of the gentle reader by the subjects or the details of their realism. The reader
knows that much was unconfessed, much unsaid.
The veil of reticence was visible, as veils always are;
but there it was, so that there was no need of another to conceal the blush of shame if a southern
maiden turned the pages.

In Mr. Young's twentieth century the veil is
much thinner, the capacity for blushing being almost lost. Uncle George Clay, the most amiable
gentleman in the book, drank a great deal when-
ever he liked to. He was the gentleman who told
the hog that he'd be a gentleman again when he
sobered up. He had driven his young wife out of the
house with her baby in terror late at night. He still
drank, but not as sottishly as of yore; and everybody
loved and admired him. Cousin Abe was a brutal
swashbuckler who dramatized his arrogant badness
of manners to a point where it was his distinguish-
ing mark as a gentleman. No one pursued agricul-

ture, everyone was rich with boundless inherit-
ances, the fields were radiant by day, and at eve
came the starlight and the nightingales. Subtitles
in Kennedy's *Swallow Barn* are "Knight Errantry,"
"A Joust at Utterance," and "The Last Minstrel";
in *Heaven Trees*, "Knights" and "Romance."

Eight years after this book was finished the opening page of *So Red the Rose* began, without a break,
with Malcolm Bedford sitting on the front porch
where, as usual after drinking a little too much, he
is writing imaginary epitaphs—inspired by the vulgar author of *Spoon River?* God forbid!—and where
his wife has black coffee brought out to clear his
head.

"And what's the objection to my head?"

"Nothing much, provided it's clear."

Malcolm, like Uncle George, has more than
enough money from a nameless source. Like Uncle
George he drinks his way through the story and is
loved and admired more for his dependency than for
his dependableness.

The tale involves the oncoming, progress, close,
and first aftermath of the Civil War in and near
Natchez. The atmosphere of Portobello and Mon-
trose is one with the atmosphere of Heaven Trees.
Certain characters are transferred and certain minor
episodes repeated. The familiar southern defects are
presented with the same affectionate indulgence and

contrasted with a social ideal which the South believed in but apparently made little effort to achieve. Business and commercial ruthlessness are ascribed to the North and condemned both for their character and their alleged origin. Life, the McGehees explained to each other, was tradition, ancestry and a system of living, and it was based upon a love of and reverence for the land. They also recognized, in all confidentiality, that they were already feeding upon a past and referring as a condition to what had seldom been more than a remote theory.

Thus the defect of this traditionalism is that it was not prevailingly real, and of its embodiment in persons that it was not markedly noble. In behalf of an agricultural thesis, which in the novel was cherished even less openly than the family silver and portraits, invading industrialism was inveighed against. But the total effect of *So Red the Rose* is comparable to the effect of certain famous southern gardens in the springtime: azaleas and camellias triumph above the weeds, and wisterias riot on high, the grandiloquent blooms of early spring; but there is a long, hot summer to follow, and the most casual provisions against the winter winds. Somewhere beyond them are depleted corn and cotton fields and eroded hillsides. Proof of the southerners' love of the land is hard to establish.

The Retrospective South

William Faulkner of Mississippi writes of the South in two veins: In one he represents a variation from the Agrarian viewpoint, writing of a defeated and outdated gentry, victims of the northern enemy, of their own natures—in which were the seeds of self-defeat—and of the hatefully successful exploiters from the poor white stratum, whose crude rapacity was too much for them. In a succession of Civil War and post–Civil War novels the conflict is developed between these two surviving elements in the South—the Sartoris family and the Snopes clan. But since the vileness of the poor-white Snopeses, starkly represented, involved degeneracy in its extremer forms, degeneracy in itself, in comfort and in squalor, has come to fill several other volumes with pimps, prostitutes, and perverts in ultimate forms of decadence. One kind of Faulkner story deals with nobility in decline, the other with animalism unrestrained.

Faulkner's writing started with the Civil War theme. One book in this series will serve as well as another. *The Unvanquished* is a set of six narratives about the Sartoris family, each complete in itself. The first four center about the old grandmother, grandson John, and John's companion and negro body servant, Ringo, during the last years of the war. The last pair center round John Sartoris, Sr., and his intrepid second cousin and second wife,

Drusilla, in earliest Reconstruction days. The unified code of the book is set by the Sartoris code, which, exacting much of itself, yet sets itself above the law. The colonel must nobly protect his family and defend his sacred soil, but he may indulge a wicked temper and a cruel tongue until they lead to his own death from a long-suffering partner whom he has converted into a deadly foe. The grandmother must be an exacting disciplinarian about petty breaches of behavior, but in behalf of an impoverished countryside she may make herself a public almoner from the proceeds of systematic forgeries. When the old lady is done to death the two boys may track down, kill, and mutilate the murderer; and when the elder Sartoris is shot to death the son, now come to manhood, may repudiate the obligation to kill the killer only by publicly putting himself in mortal peril. Drusilla, whose love has been transferred from father to son, can despise the son when she suspects him of cowardice, but can leave behind her a tribute of admiration when she flees in escape from the temptation to acknowledge as a widow the love to which she has confessed as an unfaithful wife. This is all quite rarified, but it is chivalry untainted by the gallantry of the conventional old plantation and old southern gentleman who flourished in one form or another from the days of Hopkinson Smith's Colonel Carter past Cabell's élite to Stark Young's grandiloquent and bibulous gentry. At the same time, always present in person or by implication in Faulkner's books are the crass upstarts who began their rise in carpetbagger times and have been on their dire ascent ever since.

Of the type of novels in which Faulkner deals with submarginal life he has written and with authority, condemning himself as he wrote: "I began to think of books in terms of possible money. I decided I might just as well make some of it myself. I took a little time out and speculated what a person in Mississippi would believe to be current, chose what I thought was the right answer, and invented the most horrible tale I could imagine and wrote it [*Sanctuary*] in about three weeks." The publisher protested that he could not put it in print but reconsidered after he had issued *As I Lay Dying*. Suddenly Faulkner was confronted with the galley proofs. "I think I had forgotten about *Sanctuary*, just as you might forget about anything made for an immediate purpose, which didn't come off. . . . . Then I saw that it was so terrible that there were but two things to do: tear it up or rewrite it. . . . . So I tore the galleys down and rewrote the book . . . . trying to make out of it something that would not shame *The Sound and the Fury* and *As I Lay Dying*, and I made a fair job."

As I Lay Dying, which Faulkner did not want to

shame by writing an inferior work, is the account of the death and burial of a country woman, mother of four children by her husband and one by the local preacher. It tells of the building of her coffin and the slow mid-summer progress of the funeral wagon to her home town. The journey is interrupted by flood and accident, a long detour is necessary, the heat is excessive, and the corpse corrupts until it attracts buzzards and shocks the passers-by. As the family assembles for the return trip, the widower appears with a new wife.

Sanctuary itself, the "fair job" which was undertaken as the most horrible thing the author could imagine, but which satisfied him in revised form, centers around three people: a frustrated lawyer who is trying to escape an unhappy marriage and to find himself in legitimate activity; an impotent, sadistic racketeer; and a southern college flapper, who drifts from silly insubordination into a nightmare adventure, in the course of which she is violated, half-imprisoned in a bawdy-house, apparently dragged down to utter abandonment of character and then apparently rescued and sullenly reconciled to half-imprisonment in a life of sheltered and aimless luxury.

Or consider *The Wild Palms*, Faulkner's tale of 1939 and the last to be discussed here. It is composed of two stories, or a story and its sequel, though they are related in eight alternating instalments. The events which occurred in the first involve a medical student, young and colorless when introduced. He falls in love at first sight with a young wife and mother, who is somewhat restlessly enshrined in respectability. Her Roman Catholic husband, when informed, releases her in a freedom which does not include divorce. The lovers turn vagabond, subsisting partly on stolen findings, partly on their joint earnings, his in medical technology and hers in plastic art. After nearly reaching bottom dollar they find jobs which secure ample food and shelter but restrict them to an exhausting routine. Throwing this over they encounter their sternest physical hardships, aggravated by her pregnancy, which drives him to a desperate and fatal attempt to practice an abortion and a resultant conviction to a fifty-year prison term. The husband remains doggedly generous to the lover out of respect to his wife's wishes. The lover refuses chances for escape either by flight or suicide, and pays what he regards as the price, not for his sin, but for his transitory happiness. The other story, which seems until the end of the book to be quite unrelated, and then is related only by implication, is about the experiences of the convicted lover in a flood-relief adventure of nightmare proportions, during which he is reported and recorded as drowned, returns and surrenders, and is penalized with an added ten years on a trumped-up charge of attempted escape, a burden which like his original sentence he accepts with utter stoicism.

In a long soliloquized piece of introspection delivered to a friend before the lovers escape from the bondage of security, the lover, Wilbourne, presents his and Faulkner's philosophy of life, which is in its way a perfect contemporary document for such as will subscribe to it: The times are out of joint; civilization offers nothing to commend it. The vast majority, living in desperate and unacknowledged resignation, surrender to the twin desires for money and social status. Love has no place in this world, and there is no place for religion, only for the pretense of it. Thrift and conformity reign. Security breeds the virtues that go with ease and the expensive enjoyment of the good things of life; but these virtues breed "fanaticism, smugness, meddling, fear, and worst of all, respectability." This much has been said by many from Thoreau to Sinclair Lewis; but Faulkner proceeds inexorably to his conclusion that in refuge from drabness ecstasy must be achieved in defiance of all conformity and must be paid for at whatever price life and society demand. In the course of this self-analysis it appears that Wilbourne is abandoning a career as a successful writer, a source of income to which utter need does not tempt him to resort again. Referring to his stories he says, "I had even stopped . . . . apologizing to myself. . . . . In fact I had come to really like to write them, even apart from the money. . . . . Besides, after I started writing them I learned that I had no idea of the depths of depravity of which the human invention is capable, which is always interesting——"

" 'You mean, enjoys,' McCord said."

The implication is clear that while Faulkner was writing stories about the Sartoris family, survivors of a chivalrous past, with their assumption that not to be magnanimous was to be a traitor, he recognized that the demands of something higher than respectability reduced depravity to its place as an incident and as an obstacle to a desirable life; but that when he turned to the South of the Snopeses, who proceeded on the assumption that anything was justified that got the goods and who felt no restraints because they were incapable of feeling shame, he felt that the depths of depravity were interesting and enjoyable in themselves.

To both kinds of material Faulkner has brought a skill in narration which is always remarkable and sometimes distracting; and it is not without significance that the technique is simpler and the content more lucid in the tales which have the greater normality, or that they become more intricate and elusive in the tales of abnormality; that, in short, technique becomes a compensation for content as content sinks in the scale of accepted values. It is probably also not without significance that Faulkner's novels and short stories have much of the dream quality in them. Sometimes this lies in an extraordinary lucidity of a simple but paradoxical episode, sometimes in sheer horror of nightmare intensity, and often it is in a sense of overpowering confusion and chaotic multiplicity from which one is glad to awaken. Almost always it is effective in its way.

The old Sartoris code is fitted to a method of telling stories that comes from the past. As Faulkner uses it, it is an old-fashioned mode brought down to date, stripped of the obvious and the directly expository, filled with suggestion and implication, rapid in movement, but demanding for the most part no more than alert attention to catch the whole structure or the significance of page by page or sentence by sentence. There is little narrative writing more graphic or more engrossing than "Skirmish at Sartoris" with the dual struggle of the unreconstructable southerners who can rout the carpetbaggers but cannot cope with their own womenfolk, or than "Odor of Verbena" in which young John refuses to undertake blood vengeance.

When, however, we come to the other kind of

South, the South from which the Snopeses come, and from which some of their sort have risen in fortune without rising in nature, the complexity of the telling increases. Not in *Sanctuary*, for this was written too fast to be intricately devious, but in such novels as *Light in August*, *As I Lay Dying*, and *The Wild Palms*. The characters in *Sanctuary* are hard to follow, partly because they are not made clear at the outset and partly because they are not convincing as they go on. But *As I Lay Dying* is told by fourteen narrators, some in their own character, some in Faulkner's style, and some in shifting styles. Read and then read again, they ultimately become intelligible, and they share in a unified whole. Yet when the reader has done his generous share in constructing and reconstructing the story, his reward is not in what he finds but only in having found it by the hard way of Faulkner's elusive technique.

Similarly in *The Wild Palms* there is no clear reason for the scheme of construction. The book contains two separate stories. They are either totally unrelated in character and event, or one is sequel to the other. Yet they are presented in the order A-B-A-B-A-B-A-B, and all of B is subsequent in time to all of A. Not only that, but the opening scene of A belongs in time almost at the end of that narrative, and certain of the details are utterly unintelligible until the whole has been completed, when, by checking back, they are proved to have some meaning. Not only that, but the book is obscured by sentences as complex as the total structure, anaconda sentences of which the reader soon learns that he will do well to peek at the end before he tries to follow them through all their convolutions.

There is a skill inherent in this intricacy of both wholes and parts; there is a convincing tone in the presentation of depravity; there is even a credibility in the irrational and inconsistent behavior of characters who are balanced by no controls either of habit or of conviction. If the Sartoris code is lost forever and there is nothing left us but the baseness of the Snopeses or the despair of the Wilbournes, Faulkner has "made a fair job." To revert to Hergesheimer's phrases, he has surrendered to "the assault of a persuasive discontent" and made his contribution to "a confusion of forms very like the age." Whether the discontent is irresistibly persuasive and the confusion of forms is inevitable are questions on which the reader has a right to reserve his opinion. To agree is to accept Faulkner as not only skilful but truthful; to dissent is to grant his skill but to deny him a significance beyond that to which any straw in the literary wind is entitled.

VII
Sherwood Anderson

IN HIS *Story Teller's Story* and in *Tar* Sherwood Anderson long ago told of how his feeling for life grew into something articulate and of how the story-telling gift was born and grew in him. He exercised it now as a dreamer, now as an ornate liar, now as a discontent who did not know that he was a square peg in a round hole, as for instance an advertising writer whose trade value was increased by the rumor that he had sold some fiction, though not enough to keep him alive, and a manufacturer who one day discovered that instead of selling his goods not very fast he was actually selling his soul. He was quite detached in the telling, neither vain nor proud. He gave more space to his father than to anyone else, because he understood the histrionic self-glorification that led to his story-telling, though to just the kind that the son has always abjured. For he shows that the tales he himself tells are one with the life he has lived.

These books of autobiography, like all good narrative, are records of interesting moments, moments which usually mark a release of the imagination into fields that are like as not unrelated to the facts of the instant. There is a suspicion of oil in the neighborhood, and a well is to be shot. The promoter becomes a figure of mystery and romance. His nitroglycerin brings up only a shower of mud, and he is translated into a villain about whose duplicity the imagination can linger happily. He is rather more satisfying fictive material than a successful well. The story-teller loathes the man working next to him in a nail factory and remembers a negro boxer with a quick shift and a powerful left. Daydreams of using the invincible tactics lead to the moment of picking a quarrel and the paralyzing defeat that follows. He sits with the managers of a concern for which he is to write some advertising copy. One of them has a scar almost concealed by his beard. Into the dim past fades the speaker with all his sales talk, and the "ad" writer dreams the thrilling story that accounts for the scar.

So his imagination gains sway and he begins casting round for stories to tell. They must contain an element of beauty, and the story-teller must be consciously a new product of a new land. This new land turns out to be a puzzling place, complicated by the indeterminable people who populate it. It is a country that first of all is not English, though the notion that it is has persisted for centuries. The blood is a mixture of two chief strains: the thin blue of the Puritans and the redder hues of the dreaming nations of Europe. In the mixture many elements assert themselves intermittently, which is the reason that the resultant compound is so perplexing. On the one hand the Celts and the Latins and the nations of the Far East pour their contributions into the veins of America—a love of beauty and song and mirth and the rightness of things rightly made by capable hands. They are the natural breeders of the artist who is forsworn to his devotion for form and color and the controlled ecstasy through which he can fulfil himself. They have made things of lasting beauty, built the cathedrals at Chartres and Venice and Mont-St.-Michel, and they have worshiped the Virgin. Their peoples have encouraged the artist and enjoyed his work and put up with his vagaries, not taking them too seriously.

On the other hand here are the Puritanic English, godly and self-denying and others-denying, and fatefully practical, bound always to be doing things for which the artist has no zest; so eagerly efficient that after clearing the forests and building towns they set themselves to building up a country to the glory of man, as earnest about it as the French were when they built the cathedral at Chartres to the glory of God. This was their plan, "and the affair only blew up in the process, or got perverted, because Man, even the brave and free Man, is somewhat a less worthy object than God." For in the meantime the machine age had killed the best in man.

Unconsciously, in writing of either strain in the blood of the new America, the story-teller came back to God; and in this thought his puzzlement became the greater. The heritage of the Puritans, he said to himself, was an ungodly materialism, and the heritage of the Celts and the Latins was an ungodly paganism. As for himself he had no God, the gods having been reft from him by the life about him. And yet, devout atheist, he wrote that in a dramatic moment "I had an odd, and to my own seeming, a ridiculous desire to abase myself before something not human, and so stepping into the moonlit road I knelt in the dust."

Such an atheistical weaver of tales brought his autobiography to just the right conclusion, not to be logical, but to be reasonable. For he had become an artist and wanted to round out his chronicle with that reasonableness which is an essence of art. So at the close he was sitting with a friend (James Joyce, was it?) before the cathedral in Chartres, where together they had been worshiping for days. In its presence he felt what the old craftsmen had felt who had built themselves into the fabric of it. His dream was not theirs, but the work of their hands helped him to give shape to his own dream. He could not be content to sit before the cathedral endlessly musing on old days. He must do as they did, living in the moment, in his own country, taking part in its growth. To the observer who sees him sitting before the cathedral that made him so deeply happy, he seems to have been very like those old workmen who took no thought of theology and vented their religion in work. The thoughtful man who calls himself an atheist may be a man who has not found his name for God.

Such a man, whatever his religious label or lack of one, is certain to be mobile; and the country to which he returns will not present an unchanging aspect to him. He will distrust generalizations even while he is making them. In his earlier days when the world of circumstance was crowding too insistently upon him, the thought of the machine was almost overwhelming. It was standardizing more than the product, for it was ironing out the workmen all to one size and thickness; and, as they lost their feeling for materials and their zest in the use of tools, grossness and lewdness and profanity became the pitiable outlets for their thwarted selves. Standardization has been an abused word these latter days. The story-teller used it mostly to indicate the process which ended in the outward evidence of inward dulness. Yet he shifted it in meaning just as he shifted in mood.

At one time, thinking about democracy and the machine, he saw a swarm of men shuffling out of a factory at the end of a day of meaningless repetitions. What was such a routine doing to the men and the society they belonged to? And to those other men in the directors' room with their meaningless lust for money and power? "Democracy shall spread itself out thinner and thinner, it shall come to nothing but empty mouthings in the end. . . . . The shrewd little money-getters with their cry 'democracy' on their lips shall rule for a time and then the real commoners shall come—and that shall be the worst time of all. Oh, the futile little vanity of the workers who have forgotten the meaning of cunning of hands, who have long let machines take the place of the cunning of hands!" Another American had shared this mood not long before:

> Shall all the happy shipmates then
> Stand singing brotherly?
> Or shall a haggard ruthless few
>   Warp her over and bring her to
> While the many broken souls of men
> Fester down in the slaver's pen
>   And nothing to say or do?

That is one mood; but in another the story-teller regained his confidence: "Standardization is a

phase. It will pass. The tools and materials of the
workmen cannot always remain cheap and foul. If
the machine is to survive it will come again under
the dominance of the hands of the workmen, as it
already, no doubt, is doing, in a hundred, perhaps a
thousand, unknown places. The day of rediscovery
of man by man may not be as far off as we fancy.''
This, too, that other poet had said:

> Then, perhaps, at the last day,
> They will whistle him away,
> Lay a hand upon his muzzle in the face of God and say,
> "Honor, Lord, the thing we tamed!
> Let him not be scourged or blamed,
> Even through his wrath and fierceness was thy fierce
>   wroth world reclaimed.''

He realized, however, that optimism was well
only as it was hardy enough to face the facts. There
was an America to be recognized while the struggle
was on between the machine brute and the finer
nature of man. The story-teller might escape into
the world of fancy, but even his fancy was based on
fact. And in his opinion the most salient fact about
American life was, perhaps, the kind of fancy with
which the average American enveiled himself. He
considered himself part of a heroic enterprise, a
gigantic social experiment in which he assumed
that the most unprepossessing man was a potential
hero. The sober fact that this was not true afforded

the forgotten man all the more reason for clinging to the fancy as he had been emboldened to do by a succession of fabulists from Bret Harte to Bill Hart.

So this average American, whose zest as creative tool-user was being blighted by the producing and consuming of cheap things cheaply made, was also having his imagination standardized. He had created or, more exactly, adopted a hero who was interestingly bad but reassuringly good; who was guilty of every offense in the sight of man and of God but who was capable of becoming high and fine at the utterance of the word "mother" or the appearance of a defenseless and immaculate maid. He was an agreeable fiction, but he was a dishonest fiction because he was both so much worse and so much better than the novel-readers, show-goers, and moving-picture addicts who admired him and sniffled at his nobler manifestations. He was undermining the honesty of a whole people and laying snares for the story-tellers who might be honest if left to their own devices. "As I sat in the movie house it was evident that Bill Hart was being loved by all the men, women and children sitting about, and I also want to be loved—to be a little feared and dreaded too, perhaps! 'Ah! there goes Sherwood Anderson! Treat him with respect. He is a bad man when he is aroused. But treat him kindly and he will be as gentle with you as any cooing dove!' "

Sherwood Anderson

The Anderson who had momentary flashes of desire to be the bold, bad movie hero was making more of a confession than he realized. The furtive wish is common at sight of a Cooper, Gable, Tracy, an acrobat, billiard champion, or all-American half-back. The sentimentalist is amused as it passes and goes back to selling bonds, making carpet tacks, or teaching school. The decision has usually been made for better or for worse. There has been no compounding with fate, because the thing yearned for was so remote from the thing being done.

But for Sherwood Anderson there was an actual escape. He could do both. His deliberate choice, made in front of the cathedral in Chartres, was to become the fine craftsman, working honestly with the rough material of middle-western life. It was life he was after and not plot. It was the appropriate language that he wanted to use and not literary English. He must never lose his real interest in the people around him; and when he became aware of a story pleading to be told, he must lend himself to the simple folk who lived it, or might have lived it, and believe in those people until he and they were one. But there was another way out for him when the desire burned to be bold and bad. In the very reality of his people there was an element that the story-tellers who had just preceded him had avoided —the persistence of sex feeling. He could vindicate

his artistic integrity by ruthlessly dwelling on this
and could thus be a little shocking in the name of
art. "There goes Sherwood Anderson. He can be a
lustful male when he is aroused!"

Mr. Anderson is in fact a sensitive artist, and in
his mid-career he could be sensitive to most hostile
criticism. The criticism that any of his characters
are not worthy a place in fiction hurts him. But the
criticism, when it was made, that he was a wicked
man with a wicked mind carried no such sting. As a
matter of fact, he was early among many moderns to
invite it with a somewhat Whitmanic insistence on
wearing his hat indoors or out and sounding his
Freudian yawp over the roofs of the world or raising the roof if he happened to be in the bedroom
under the eaves. It was too conscious, like the re-
movable front of O'Neill's house under the elms.

In *Winesburg, Ohio* and in *Many Marriages*, which
belong in his earlier output, Mr. Anderson was re-
acting against the Victorian conspiracy of silence,
doing his share to restore the balance of the age by
displaying some unbalance of his own. The problem
looms hardly as large as he suggested, nor was he
as morbid as some of his offended critics insisted. A
flood of later books by younger writers make his
work seem decidedly inoffensive if not pallid. In
writing of sex experience he was seldom circumstantial and never sickly. There was "a deal of cir-

cumambient hocus-pocus'' among certain of his contemporaries who coquetted with the theme; and as one looks back to the twenties and around at the forties, a corrected impression leads us to

> think of what he never said
> Of women—which, if taken all in all
> With what he did say, would buy many horses.

Here then are the two main interests in Sherwood Anderson, both developing in his early career: the theme of man and woman and the theme of man and the machine. One day they were to be interwoven, but at present they had no clear relation in his thinking. We must turn back again to the machine. In his earlier novels, and particularly in *Marching Men*, he was preoccupied by the problems of the industrial order and a sense of responsibility for setting it right. Society was chaos, the workmen were a wronged body, but a restoration of the rhythm of life would set all things in their places in a sentimental millennium. *Marching Men* seemed like a compound of Rousseau and Zola, in which Rousseau did him no great service. One reads a passage like this and is not stirred: "Chicago is one vast gulf of disorder. Here is the passion for gain, the very spirit of the bourgeoisie gone drunk with desire. The result is something terrible. Chicago is leaderless, purposeless, slovenly, down at the heels. And back of Chicago lie the cornfields that are not

disorderly. There is hope in corn. Spring comes and
the corn is green." This was commonplace enough,
a far cry from the sort of writing he aspired to in the
person of the hero of his tale, which was to make
his true note heard above the hubbub of voices, not
the echo of other men's thoughts. Mr. Anderson did
not sound this true note of his own until he became
more interested in what was happening in the minds
of his characters than in what was going on outside
their bodies. They were the same people surrounded
by the same conditions, but they were no longer
mainly significant because they were creatures of
circumstance. They might even be such victors over
circumstance as Sponge Martin.

In *Dark Laughter* Sponge is unremarkable to look
at or listen to; he appears to be just one more man in
a factory, inactive, unprotesting, contented. He
lives in a little, old, converted barn on the edge of
town, with his little, old, companionable wife.
They eat and sleep together, they share the occasional sprees that they call "going fishing." Sponge
is a competent workman whose hands have become
so skilled that he does not need to pay attention to
them as his mind runs on in vague memories and his
tongue in interminable talk. To the restless man at
the next bench Sponge is a problem. Is he never dis-
contented? Do his job, his wife, his home, satisfy
him? Is he satisfied with life? "Bruce decided that

the old man was not necessarily self-satisfied. With him being satisfied or not satisfied did not count. . . . . He liked the skill of his own hands. That gave him something to rest on in life. . . . . As to his old woman—there was a thing her man could do better than most men. He rested in that fact and his wife rested in him. The man and the woman had stayed within the limits of their powers, had moved freely within a small but clear circle of life." The pair are not merely described and dismissed in *Dark Laughter;* they appear and reappear throughout the story. They are an undercurrent in the book, just as they and their kind are an undercurrent in the stream of American life. Many of Anderson's contemporaries have poured out their scorn on characters who have not known enough to be unhappy. This portrait of the Martin couple, painted without prejudice, is one of the best in recent literature—a notable picture.

The difference between *Marching Men* and *Dark Laughter* is parallel to the difference between Anderson the manufacturer and Anderson the developing author. When he had passed from thinking of men as slaves to the industrialism from which he had escaped, and had come to thinking of men and women as living in a world of primary experiences so vital that their inciting causes faded into unimportance, the factory lost interest as a factory and

(125)

the slum as a slum, though they might be used as backgrounds. The one matter that counted was to catch the moments when people were really living and to find the words that could record them.

These were the rare moments when individuals were able to surmount or penetrate or break down the walls by which they were cut off from their fellows. The metaphor, once noted, recurs insistently in Anderson's pages. The wall, the wall, the wall. Only now and again do humans come into each other's real presences. Partners, plotters, husbands and wives, are all held apart by impalpable barriers. "Men had themselves built the walls and now stood behind them, knowing dimly that beyond the walls there was warmth, light, air, beauty, life in fact— while at the same time and because of a kind of madness in themselves, the walls were constantly being built higher and stronger." In a sketch called "The Man's Story" he expounded this in prose and he put it into verse in a poem which ends,

"Do you see this hand? Suppose it held a knife that could cut down through all the falseness in you. Suppose it could cut down through the sides of buildings and houses where thousands of people now lie asleep.

"It would be something worth thinking about if the fingers of this hand gripped a knife that could cut and rip through all the ugly husks in which millions of lives are enclosed."

However, the wall still faced him and the machine still faced him and he was still baffled. A *Dial* prize had paid his way to Europe where he had encountered James Joyce and Gertrude Stein, who were not concerned with machines. Later he had spent some time with William Faulkner. Now he had solid royalties from *Dark Laughter*—real money for the first time in his life as a writer. With it he bought a sizable house and two country newspapers in Virginia and set out in the footsteps of William Allen White. It was a picturesque thing to do, and he was not unqualified for editorship. He liked folks, and he was master of an easy style; but running newspapers on both sides of the political fence in the same town was not a career for him; it was only a journalistic adventure, hardly more than a literary stunt. He was making copy, as he did in the excellent books of autobiography with which a story-teller can pad out his work, as he can with the printing of his notebooks, which Anderson also did. Let him give his own account of himself:

"I had written of the period of change. I had been a writer for twenty years. . . . . I had at least not gone to Paris, to sit eternally in cafes, talking of art. I had stuck and yet, as that woman pointed out to me, all my efforts had been efforts to escape.

Time and again I had told the story of the man crushed and puzzled by the age of the machine. I had told the story until I was tired of telling it. I had retreated from the city to the town, from the town to the farm."

The woman who pointed this out to him charged him with being a coward, twitted him with over-emphasizing sex, declared that the machine was as mighty as love and maybe even mightier. Whether this woman is a figment or a fact, Anderson was re-called to his original pair of themes, and in a little book called *Perhaps Women*, a set of assembled frag-ments, he tried to combine them. The machine is crushing man. It can't crush women because they have an "inner life," which seems to be potential maternity. The women, whether in factory or out, do not want the factory men for mates. "There will be no lovers. There will be only husbands [this is a Faulkner thesis]. . . . . If money and the machine continue to rule men's lives, then we shall have to surrender maleness." This is the sort of oversimpli-fication which arrives at a *reductio ad absurdum*. Still puzzled by economic developments, whipped by the contempt of the challenging woman, and still wishing to be a "little worm in the fair apple of Progress"—the bold, bad man in disguise—An-derson spins a cocoon from his own vitals: All males work with machines; all machine-workers are nothing but machine-tenders; all machine-tenders are devitalized by the monotony and speed of their work; all women react alike to all males.

As an artist, Sherwood Anderson has now and again drawn characters who have human traits for which the big word "universal" is sometimes used. The artisan, Sponge Martin, who can paint wheels in the wagon factory, secure in his skill, is an illustration. The artist supplies the individual, and the reader may do the generalizing. But when Anderson steps out of the studio into the study and attempts to generalize as sociologist or economist he is beyond his depth. As an artist he has a native gift; but there is no native endowment of broad information for anyone, and generalizations without facts and balance and control are silly when they are made with lyric enthusiasm and a disregard for statistics.

Anderson demonstrates once more the difference between story-teller and essayist in his novel *Kit Brandon* as he creates a character, places her in definite situations, and makes her at once exceptional and reasonably convincing. For Kit is a woman, though a superwoman. She is superior to her mountaineer parentage, to the factory people with whom for a while on her way up she has contacts but no connections, to the bootleggers whom she joins, and to the federal agents she eludes or outwits. Everywhere she moves she is an outlaw. She uses her native wit, her courage, and her body to gain her ends. Like her author's, all her efforts are at escape; and at the end of the tale she is still in flight, not from the law, but from herself and her past. Kit is a credible character, a special product of a special period in America; and in her unique way she is a type of twentieth-century womanhood in her self-sufficiency and high defiance. To that extent she is a literary creation, but not a sociological fact to multiply by a million and generalize from—the woman who is not crushed by the machine.

Kit Brandon, as this is written four years after it, is the last item in the Anderson output. It is an output covering twenty-odd years in which there is no clear progress. It ends about where it began. A gift for narrative-writing seemed to offer great promise at the start, but there has been no progress in fulfilment. Anderson is as puzzled and baffled and indeterminate at the end as Kit Brandon is in the closing sentence with which he dismisses her: "She would get into some sort of work that did not so separate her from others. There might be some one other puzzled and baffled young one with whom she could make a real partnership in living."

VIII

Theodore Dreiser

THEODORE DREISER is the author of six novels. One of these was published and withdrawn in 1900; four appeared between 1911 and 1915; one, and far the most popular one, came out in 1925. Before the publication of the first he was a newspaper reporter; up to the appearance of the second he was magazine editor. Interspersed since then among his novels, short stories, poems, and plays are a succession of personal reminiscences, political and social studies, essays, and books of description and travel. Thus though his reputation rests on his work as a novelist, the greater part of his writing has been in prose exposition of himself, his country, and life in general. In his career as a writer there has been a steady progress from pure narration, past expository narrative, to unadulterated exposition. He has always been something of a crusader.

Dreiser, like his antithesis, Cabell, was under a heavy initial debt to his hostile critics, for both came into general celebrity by the avenue of notoriety. In 1900 Dreiser's *Sister Carrie* was issued and suppressed by a New York publisher—the same year in which Zola's *Fecundity* was published and widely circulated. According to Dreiser, "we were not used then in America to calling a spade a spade, particularly in books. We had great admiration for Tolstoi and Flaubert and Balzac and De Maupassant at a distance . . . . but mostly we had been schooled to the literature of that refined company of English sentimental realists who told us something about life but not everything." When *Jennie Gerhardt* appeared eleven years later, *Sister Carrie* was resuscitated, giving Dreiser the advantage of a twofold approach to the public. People were startled. Whether they were delighted or perturbed depended on artistic and moral predilections, but they were all agog. In the meanwhile the interim had done much to sophisticate the American reader, but fortunately for Dreiser not quite enough to make him acceptable as a matter of course. So fresh objections were raised, as they were later to the Cowperwood tales. Dreiser was barred hither and yon from school and village libraries; and his reputation was established. The Caliban of contemporary fiction!

As this tempest was taking its course, the career of Ferdinand was also developing. Cabell had been writing voluminously for the periodicals, but without wide recognition. Novels, tales, and poems were coming along from a comparatively unknown publishing house. But when *Jurgen* appeared and was suppressed through the efforts of a society for the suppression of vice, which branded it as phallic literature, collectors paid as high as forty dollars for copies; critic after critic began discussing not *Jurgen* alone but the whole course and value of Cabell's work; Hugh Walpole paid him the tribute of a bookful of appraisal; and when the legal ban was removed, *Jurgen* was displayed in the window of every enterprising bookseller, and the author was put in position to enlarge the herd at Dumbarton Grange. Ferdinand had made his entrance in the center of the stage, and ten thousand Mirandas were enthralled.

But the jury of critics was divided on Caliban. By 1915 Stuart Sherman had declared that Dreiser had told just two things about his favorite character, Frank Cowperwood: that he had a rapacious appetite for wealth and for women. The books about him, he wrote, were in effect huge sandwiches "composed of slices of business alternating with erotic episodes." H. L. Mencken retorted on the "critical imbecility which detects naught save a tom-cat in Frank Cowperwood." And Carl Van Doren, who was more interested in understanding Dreiser than in fighting about him, said that he was a mystic who employed the gestures of a realist.

Those who were having Dreiser held up to them as a morbid anatomist, a moral ghoul obsessed with animalism, might well have opened a direct acquaintance by reading *Twelve Men*. The book would have supplied a quite conventional point of departure; for almost every subject of these dozen portraits, to quote the author, "deliberately and of choice holds fast to many, many simple human things, and rounds out life, or would, in a natural, normal, courageous, healthy way." Peter is a gay lover of life who reaches his self-fulfilment as the incarnation of faithful domesticity; Charlie Potter is "just a good man, that's all"; Paul Dresser is vast, jovial, good-hearted unselfishness in the flesh; Dr. Gridley is the servant of the whole countryside. As portraits these men are merely set against picturesque backgrounds; but in the six novels, which represent the author's most ambitious attempt to present life, men and women are placed in the midst of a multitudinous world, and become manikins played with by internal and external forces which they can never control and to which they are usually unable to adjust themselves. It is a grim world, but the grimness arises less from the sight and thought of social hardship than from the consciousness of ruthless, supernatural forces. Whether the central characters are externally successful or not, success is not an end or even a resting-point for them. It is a wave crest on a turbulent stream.

In fact, the symbol for Dreiser as for Mark Twain is that raft on which Huckleberry Finn floated—a raft without directive power of its own on a full current with a shifting channel; essentially unstable, it could afford no basis for security, no point of departure, for departure implies at least momentary anchorage. Like Mark Twain and like Whitman, Dreiser has had no clearly defined philosophy but has been a continual asker of questions. "I am one of those curious persons who cannot make up their minds about anything." As a youth he had been like the reporter he tells of in *Nigger Jeff* who up to the time of covering a lynching assignment had been a "rather self-sufficient youth who was inclined to be of the turn of mind which sees in life only a fixed and ordered process of rewards and punishments," but who came at the end of that day's work to the conviction that "it was not always exact justice that was meted out to all, and that it was not so much the business of the writer to indict as to interpret." In another passage Dreiser recorded this shift in point of view in terms still more direct: "About this time I read the *Data of Ethics* and *First Principles* of Herbert Spencer. They nearly killed me, took every shred of belief away from me; showed me that I was a chemical atom in a whirl of unknown forces; the realization clouded my mind. I felt the rhythm of life, but the central fact to me was that the whole thing was unknowable—incomprehensible. I went into the depths and I am not sure that I have ever gotten entirely out of them."

In the sense of uncertainty about the underlying laws of life, he has been an agnostic, like the later Mark Twain; but in his incessant effort to reach solid ground and his desire to tread confidently on it, he has been more like Whitman, and even Emerson. He has been perplexed by the "mad chaos of fraud, frivolity and hoggishness," but much of the time he has not been dismayed by it. He has seemed to think that he has subscribed to the mechanistic theory—popularly Darwinism—"survival of the species, adaptation, and all their evolution terms," a theory which regards the individual as helpless; yet over and over he has betrayed the suspicion that will not down in him, that there is an inward, impelling force, pushing mankind upward as well as onward.

Again and again he has explicitly denied the existence of justice and morality, yet he has seldom stopped groping to find what he has called "the equation inevitable." The earth, he has said, is populated with giants and pigmies; the giants eat the pigmies when they can. They leave devastation in their train, and, in strange irony, monuments to

beauty, too. Yet, after all, he falls back on law in
an Emersonian resort to the principle of compensation. "In the end a balance is inevitably struck
wherein the mass subdues the individual or the individual the mass—for the time being. For, behold,
the sea is ever dancing or raging. In the meantime
there have sprung up social words and phrases expressing a need of balance—of equation. These are
right, justice, truth, morality, an honest mind, a
pure heart—all words meaning a balance must be
struck." In characterizing his Twelve Men he added
to this list of nouns the adjectives "natural, normal, courageous, healthy." The concepts are personal, therefore, as well as social. The ideas which
Dreiser rejected with his mind he clung to by instinct. The social words, repudiate them though he
might, are the nearest substitute for the Rock of
Ages that he has ever found; and as events have
proved, he was continually to clamber back to them
as the sea has danced and raged, never more persistently than in his latest novel, *An American
Tragedy*.

The central characters in the Dreiser novels are
all driven by inner compulsions. Sister Carrie, from
Columbia City, Wisconsin, is started on what a publisher's protesting wife regarded as the road to ruin;
but borne on the tide of circumstance she is lifted

out of penurious labor and out of the pitfalls of love without benefit of clergy to success on the stage and to a condition of life in which there are no devastating traces of the upward struggle. At the end she is anything but a stricken soul. Sitting in luxurious quarters, she is still young and still lovely, knowing neither surfeit nor complete contentment; dreaming and doomed to dream always of a happiness she will never quite attain. The substitution of impulse control for ethical control, however, lifted the novel out of the pattern which had heretofore shaped the course of stories in terms of virtue and vice, victim and villain. Carrie, the eternal feminine, is not an innocent victim and need not pay a penalty for conscious transgression. Drouet, the seducer, is a cheerful, irresponsible drifter who drifts out of the picture in due time, and Hurstwood, the second lover, goes to ruin not for his villainy but because of persisting flabby indecision. None has made a particular, decisive choice; all are creatures of accidental circumstance. Carrie prospers because she is the embodiment of a primary force in life, the feminine impulse to please and allure. And the novel is constructed to demonstrate not the rewards and punishments in which Dreiser no longer believed but the haphazard unpredictability in life of which he had become convinced. It affords, he explains "an illustration of the devious way by which one who feels rather than reasons, may be led in the pursuit of beauty." Jennie Gerhardt in another concluding passage comes to the same opinion: "All of us are more or less pawns. We're moved about like chessmen by circumstances over which we have no control." The abrogation of ethical controls had its repercussions in the subsequent debate between what Stuart Sherman called the Party of Culture and the Party of Nature.

In the projected "trilogy of desire" of which only two were completed, *The Financier* and *The Titan*, Dreiser went on to the study of the master-passions for possessions and power. Cowperwood, central figure, is born to conquest, squanderer of many fortunes and many loves. The poetic justice of literary tradition would do away with him as it did with Hurstwood; but the last glimpses of him reveal him not punished, but rewarded with his latest love and setting out for fresh victories in new financial fields. The American scene, the urban scene of big business in alliance with boss politics, is presented here in minutest detail. Dreiser invented nothing. Charles T. Yerkes, Philadelphia, and Chicago supplied his materials, and the newspapers and court records made them available. In *Tragic America* (1931), a book of essays not to be confused with *An American Tragedy* (1925), Dreiser waxed shrill and semi-hysterical over the social injustices for which capital was responsible, but in the Cowperwood chronicles he was of the opinion expressed in *Hey Rub-a-Dub-Dub* (1920) on "The American Financier." This character is a catlike threader of ways between laws, public opinion, and theories of morals, who is cold and selfish to the last degree but ultimately useful at that. For he makes his way by studying the needs of the multitude and profits by satisfying them with the largest possible returns to himself. He not only serves the public in materially improving their conditions, but he also in his very deviousness and rapacity throws some light on "this strange phantasmagory called existence" and has been worth his salt for this contribution to human knowledge. "For myself, then, I cannot say that personally or socially the American, or any other financier, as I have investigated him, is not as satisfactory as may be, all things considered. . . . . One thing is sure: the individual cannot wholly understand the mass, nor the mass the individual. Both have their significance, their place."

Cowperwood is presented, then, without prejudice as a type. He knows as a youth that his gift is to manipulate other men. He has a zest for life equal to that of any man on the soil; but his place is in the town, his medium is in finance, his pawns are the men whom he may either use or sweep off the board. He has developed a skill in which he delights, and he delights in being an instrument of destiny even though an accident may have made him so. Dreiser thus follows the threader of ways, bears testimony to his usefulness, admires his acquisitive gifts as long as they are successfully exercised, and is as cold and vicariously selfish as the figure he is studying, powerful, yet powerless to control his own energies.

An American Tragedy was written out of the depths from which Dreiser had never escaped after reading Herbert Spencer. Clyde Griffiths, he took immense pains to show, is a chemical atom in a whirl of unknown forces, a bundle of susceptibilities played on by outer influences. Some of his natural responses are inborn, some the results of experience. He is not redeemed by the "balance" to which Dreiser alluded when discussing the social order; never reinforced by the "natural, normal, courageous, healthy" stimuli which enabled the Twelve Men to round out their lives. No positive motive can defend Clyde long against any demand of the senses— not even a cool ambition which will lead him to forgo a near desire for a remoter reward. Sister Carrie and Jennie Gerhardt, Frank Cowperwood and Witla, the artist, were all the agents of inner, driving forces. Clyde is never an agent; he is always an instrument; and he is not presented as either weak or wicked, simply as the son of his father and the product of his upbringing.

In the circumstances, which therefore are all-powerful, he drifts from one set of accidental conditions to another. Many of them open opportunities which he loses because he can never resist the external lures, for which the old-fashioned name is temptations. So when he has resolved on murder of the girl he has seduced as the sole escape from an intolerable dilemma, he loses courage at the crucial moment, and his intended victim becomes the victim of an accident for which, nevertheless, he pays the death penalty.

Dreiser surrounds this story with a shadowy background. The long tale opens with a little tableau of family evangelists in a crowded city, holding a service and distributing tracts as the multitude floods past. It closes with a replica of the same scene. After Clyde's death sentence has been passed his godly mother tries as she may to raise the money needed for a legal appeal, raising part of the sum but not enough. Her plea for clemency from the governor also fails. Circumstances are too strong for her and for the God who seems indifferent to her prayers for the life of her boy. A devoted clergyman has no better success in his attempt to save the boy's soul. Clyde, bewildered, debates with himself until he is in doubt as to his own degree of guilt, signs a conventional confession composed by the minister, asserts that he is convinced of God's forgiveness, and even yet goes to the electric chair in doubt and perplexity. The novel arrives at a climax of religious agnosticism.

At the same time it is an attempt at a document in scientific naturalism. Dreiser's statement often, and always his implication, is that the individual— Clyde the hedonist, his parents, religious dogmatists, his philistine-manufacturer uncle, any other character in whom Dreiser displays an active interest—is portrayed as a calculable and predictable person whose actions can be reckoned as responses to external stimuli. Dreiser inclines to simplify the number and the nature of the factors in his equations. To him they are all determinable and all constants. The single unpredictable element is as to what influence or stimulus will be released at any given moment. If you know what it is, you know what the reaction will be. But as a matter of fact you do not know what whimsy or chance will confront character A (who is a compound of many characteristics) with force x or force y or force z as he rounds any given corner in his career. Consequently, therefore, though the actions and the total career are all determinable in theory, they are unpredictable in reality on account of the accidental sequence of circumstances. The scientific light is thus a will-o'-the-wisp which leads one hither and yon in the antic play of its own elusiveness. It is the predicament in which any biological determinist inevitably leaves us.

It was "De Maupassant, Jr." who, according to Dreiser, "seemed finally to grasp the theory I had, or at least to develop a method of his own which was quite as satisfactory to me." This method was not satisfactory to anyone with a sense of form, for, with the exception of his last novel, his long stories have little structure save that of accretion. For the formlessness of the novels the cue is perhaps supplied in a further comment on young De Maupassant, that he was "no namby-pamby scribbler of the old happy-ending, pretty-nothing school of literary composition." The brute fact is that Dreiser never achieved a technique of narrative writing either in architectonics or in style. If there are happy endings in none of his tales, there is tragic ending only in the latest. As a rule he has written to a theme rather than to a conclusion of a plot. At a little distance from one of his stout books memory makes clear a kind of direction in it and through it; but a reader in the midst of one needs a clear head to maintain a sense of anything more than a whirling, turbulent, on-crowding tide, covered with flotsam and jetsam. In *The Financier* and *The Titan*, for example, there is no fusing of either of the cities into a defined set of characters through whom the main elements are

represented. One experience after another introduces hitherto unmentioned men and women. The
story moves only as the most erratic of lives, for as a
rule the people with whom a man will be some day
involved come gradually into his consciousness before they share in his destiny. Yet halfway through
The Titan, and long after Cowperwood has begun to
play with political pawns, he comes to a point at
which he needs to deal with more powerful men.
Chapter xxxv opens: "In the first and second wards
of Chicago at this time were two men . . . . who for
picturesqueness of character and sordidness of atmosphere could not be equalled elsewhere in the
city, if in the nation at large." Several thousand
words of characterization ensue. It is typical
Dreiserian casualness of composition.

This untrammeled desire to explain is accompanied by a regard for detail in itself which often
shows no regard for its relevance. The reader gains
nothing from the information that the Griffiths'
mission "was situated in that part of Kansas City
which lies north of Independence Boulevard and
west of Troost Avenue, the exact street or place
being called Bickel, a very short thoroughfare opening off Missouri Avenue, a somewhat lengthy but
no less nondescript highway," nor from the fact
that the attorney who prosecuted Clyde for murder
had been "able to marry the daughter of a local

druggist of some means, and two children had been born to them." This zest for explanation of the total recall type is naturally harnessed with an almost total inability to suggest. An epilogue expounds the trend of a story. Interjected comments expound character after character and action after action. Parentheses interpolate cautions against missing points that are, if anything, too obvious. Dreiser is a Flemish painter capable of spending two weeks on a broom handle; capable, however, of the patience but not of the nicety of execution, for, while he is piling up his vast accumulations of detail, he writes often clumsily, often downright badly. "He wondered when, if ever, this story was to culminate, let alone he write it." It is a perfect commentary on his own structure and style. No Hamlet could ever have said to Dreiser, "More matter and less art."

Yet scattered here and there along his pages are passages of rhythmic beauty; as for example from *Hey Rub-a-Dub-Dub:* "What has impressed me most about life, always, is the freshness and newness of everything, the perennial upwelling of life in every form; the manner in which, as age steals on for some, youth, new, innocent, inexperienced, believing, takes charge, its eyes alight with aspiration, its body ablaze with desire. . . . . Does the bit of thread or pattern that we see here now, show the least evidence of wear or tear? Is not the race as new and fresh as ever? We rise betimes, and the ancient sunlight streams fresh and strong and *new* into our passing window—this window, which, in a few years, will be as forgotten and as unrecoverable as we ourselves shall be."

This is Emersonian in tone as well as in quality; for Dreiser's philosophy was for long a balance between Emerson's and Mark Twain's, and in its vein of hope much nearer to the Concord optimist's than to the pessimist's of Stormfield. Dreiser is comparable to Emerson again in his insistence on the right of the individual to live his own life, casting behind him all conformity. Here is a passage from each. Assign them if you can. "If you maintain a dead church, contribute to a dead Bible society, vote with a great party, either for the government or against it, spread your table like base housekeepers —under all these screens I have difficulty to detect the precise man you are." "Not to cling too pathetically to a religion or a system of government or a theory of morals or a method of living, but to be ready to abandon at a moment's notice, is the apparent teaching of the ages." Their views even on the obligation of person to person are not in conflict. Says Emerson: "If you are noble, I will love you; if you are not, I will not hurt you or myself by hypocritical attentions. If you are true, but not in the same truth with me, cleave to your companions;

(147)

I will seek my own. I do this not selfishly but humbly and truly." Dreiser could say no more. Yet, in his essay on "Love" Emerson developed just the distinction between himself and his uncouth successor, while giving a character to the latter's work: "Everything is beautiful seen from the point of intellect, or as truth. But all is sour if seen from experience. Details are melancholy; the plan is seemly and noble. In the actual world—the painful kingdom of time and place—dwell canker and care and fear."

In this painful kingdom Dreiser has apparently completed his massive and hard-wrought work as a novelist. Behind there was a wistful yearning for something better, something more postive. Rejecting a religious dogma after long struggles, he seems to have found some comfort in an economic dogma, the doctrines of Karl Marx. Dreiser's six novels, we should recall, the last of which appeared in 1925, represent only a minor fraction of what he has written. Of the publications since then five volumes are based on personal experience, including *Dreiser Looks at Russia* (1928); and one, *The Tragedy of America* (1931), is a series of observations from the Marxian viewpoint on economic conditions in the United States. In this, to insure "equitable consumption," he advocates a benevolent despotism, with power to confiscate fortunes, to own and operate basic industries, and to control prices. The implication is clear that in place of his agnosticism as a writer of novels and his belief that man is a puppet of fate, he has substituted omniscience as a social philosopher and belief that the common welfare can be assured by a communist dictatorship. As the theory of his novels is out of harmony with the theory of effectual communism it became imperative either that Dreiser write a different kind of novel or abandon the writing of fiction. He has done the latter, and wisely, for his gift was to write of America as he could see it in detail, and the novel to fit his new gospel would have led him into romantic prophecy for which he has no talent.

IX
Willa Cather

IF ONE were to speculate on the literary output likely from a woman born in Virginia, diploma'd from a western state university in the 1890's, schooled in an eastern newspaper office, and graduated from the staff of a popular monthly with metropolitan headquarters and a national circulation, it would be safe to look for some copiousness of material and some breadth of sympathy. These are characteristics of Miss Cather's work. Probably they are accounted for by her experience; at any rate they are true of her output. The temptation is strong to pursue the theory that Miss Cather is the product of her changing backgrounds, for her life and works are so typically related. More often than not maturing artistry comes to its own by slow degrees, starting with conventional form and subject matter and tardily arriving at individual style and substance. That accounts for Fielding's imposing array of early comedies, Scott's excursions into poetic romance, Poe's Byronic *Tamerlane* and *Politian*, and Hawthorne's contributions to the sentimental annuals. Age and achievement lead genuine creative ability back to the fundamentals and into the literary form in which it may best express itself. This is the progression through which Miss Cather has passed, one of the very few writers in America of her generation not to lose both energy and direction in her later career.

Her first book was a typical "slender volume" of verse published in 1903 when poetry in the United States was in most hands a pleasant parlor accomplishment. The reprint of twenty years later, even with its additions, is still slender in both size and significance. There are verses of homely sentiment, classical echoes, Shakesperean, Arthurian, Italian, Provençal verses of allusion, reminiscences of travel, laments for lost loves and lost youth, and among them all three or four bits that are unbookish, with the breath of the prairies in them. Next, two years later, appeared *The Troll Garden*, seven stories—several of them stories of artists' colonies, painters, musicians, and music-lovers in New York, Boston, and London; but among them are three with reference to western life, with one grim picture of a little Kansas town to which a sculptor is brought for burial, condemned in life as in death by the sordid villagers. Then in Miss Cather's output—after a seven-year interval which seems to have been absorbed in editorial routine—came two volumes, international or transatlantic, suggesting that she was to follow the paths often traversed by Henry James and Edith Wharton. All the books so far were obviously the work of a writer who had grown up in arid rural surroundings, who was thrilled by all the reaches of beauty in studio and concert hall, and who was allured by the engaging artificialities of polite metropolitan life. The only life that occupied Miss Cather thus far was a life of aesthetic self-realization. This was her apprentice period.

She was ready for a shift in emphasis now, the focus of her attention shifting from the happy enjoyment of self-realization to the harrowing struggle toward that end. There was a change in locale too, for in the three stories which established her reputation—*O Pioneers* (1913), *The Song of the Lark* (1915), and *My Antonia* (1918)—she came far closer to a particular phase of western life, the alien immigrant on American soil, than anyone who had preceded her. The novels about Alexandra Bergson, Thea Kronberg, and Antonia Shimerda are about the transplanted European. In them, and especially in the first and last, are the prairie farm and the prairie town. In the first looms the fine figure of Alexandra, masterful, too magnanimous to be understood, doomed to spiritual solitude among her own people, but indomitable. Through the gentle melancholy of the closing lines glows an abiding

strength. In⌐ the second, Thea, equally single-
minded and equally poised, succeeds on the stage as
Alexandra succeeds on the plains. Through the two
Miss Cather identifies the spirit of the pioneer with
the spirit of the creative artist, ignoring the lesser
figures in the epic of the frontier, just as she ignores
orchestra, chorus, and stagehands in the triumph
of the opera singer. From the last of the three tales
emerges Antonia, apotheosis of the pioneer woman,
Martha glorified on the frontier, a flood of life, il-
lumined at the end in a sunset gleam against the
background of field and furrow in what had been
the open prairie.

Of the three, *The Song of the Lark*, the chronicle of
Thea Kronberg, is the least effective, perhaps for the
reason that it is most explicitly concerned with the
struggle for artistic success. Thea, daughter of a
complacent country parson, and of a prolific and instinctively wise mother, grows up a solitary in the
midst of a crowded household in a gossipy small
town. By natural gravitation she finds her most
congenial companions in a broken, half-ostracized
German music master and in a song-loving colony
of Mexican outcasts. To please her father, whom
she has no desire to offend or estrange, she plays the
hymns at the midweek prayer meetings, though she
gains no relief there from the muffling, numbing
daily clamor about her; and she always reads late

after the recital of prayers and "experiences," yearning more avidly than ever to live with zest and to achieve some real happiness.

Under the old master's monitions she toils doggedly. An instinct responds natively to his precept that "nothing is far and nothing is near if one desires. The world is little, people are little, human life is little. There is only one big thing—desire. And before it, when it is big, all is little." She need only to look within herself to recognize what he means when he declares, "The secret—what makes the rose to red, the sky to blue, the man to love—in der Brust, in der Brust it is, und ohne dieses giebt es keine Kunst, keine Kunst!" Toward this Parnassian art, then, she aspires. Leaving home, eking out a livelihood in the cities, accepting discouragement and rebuff, undeterred by lovers or even by love itself, she comes through at last to a success whose chief reward is less in gold or plaudits than in a sense of fidelity to her own high purpose.

In the end she has learned of the "inevitable hardness of human life," but also of the richness of reward that comes with creative expression. And in the end, too, she realizes once more the lesson of the old German that nothing is far and nothing is near; for with the world at her feet she discovers that it was potentially hers when she set out from the home town with her little legacy. "I shall always measure things by that six hundred dollars, just as I measure high buildings by the Moonstone stand-pipe. . . . . There is no work of art so big that it was not once all contained in some youthful body. . . . . Art is only a way of remembering youth."

In *My Antonia* there is no material reward. Antonia is a Bohemian immigrant of less than mediocre parentage, whose sole inheritance is a wholesome, hearty, clear-eyed courage. Brought up in the uses of adversity, she finds but one natural outlet; that, among her own people, is a "kind of hearty joviality, a relish of life, not over-delicate, but very invigorating." This flourishes only among the folk who are held in contempt by the respectables of the community. The dominant element are akin to the dominants of Spoon River and Gopher Prairie and Winesburg, Ohio, and to the selectmen of Friendship Village. "The life that went on in them seemed to me made up of evasions and negations; shifts to save washing and cleaning, devices to propitiate the tongue of gossip. This guarded mode of existence was like living under a tyranny. Peoples' speech, their voices, their very glances, became furtive and repressed. Every individual taste, every natural appetite, was bridled by caution. The people asleep in their houses, I thought, were trying to live like mice in their own kitchens; to make no noise, to leave no trace, to slip over the surface of things in the dark. The growing piles of cinders and ashes in the backyards were the only evidence that the wasteful, consuming process of life went on at all."

Though Antonia has no spark of creative energy, she feels the artist's desire to live a full, free life. She falls in love with a cheap seducer, and on what she thinks is to be her honeymoon she is abandoned to become an unmarried mother. Later she marries a good, dull man, brings up a big family, and in the play of her native courage arrives at a very homely, old-fashioned fulfilment of life. "That is happiness —to be dissolved in something complete and great." Antonia's achievement rests on the completeness of her dedication to her task. In her contented domesticity Miss Cather offered a modern variation on an old theme. In the pages of Mrs. Stowe, or even of Mrs. Deland, the latter stages of Antonia's career would have been presented as steps in abnegation, surrender to a sense of duty in the vale of tears which would be rewarded by a mansion prepared on high. By many contemporary novelists it would be treated as a complete defeat, with no compensation either here or hereafter. But Miss Cather, with all her zest for studio life, retained an imaginative regard for four walls and a hearthstone and the vital experience of mothering a family.

In the presentation of these three women of heroic possibilities Miss Cather fell short of completeness

because of a reason which divides itself into two:
She is a Nebrasko-Virginian, and she was writing of
immigrant people. That means, for one thing, that
she knew her people only as well as they could be
known through sympathetic observation. They are
idealized, interpreted as creative personalities, vest-
ed with the characteristics of the artists whom Miss
Cather knew by nature as well as by observation.
And it means, for another thing, since she knew her
immigrants through sympathetic observation, that
when sympathy and observation fell into conflict,
sympathy triumphed. She felt the kindliness of an
indulgent literary parent and was unwilling to resign them to their fates. She did not, therefore, record the sacrifice of the individual pioneer as the
pioneer army conquered the plains, though she allowed her fictive offspring to stray often into the
last ditches of near-defeat before she served as coun-
terleader of relief parties in a series of providential
rescues. What she lacked was the hardihood to submit to her material—scrupulous realism, the con-
scientious exactitude of the court witness, and an
unwavering resolve to follow the implications of
the testimony wherever it might lead.

After *My Antonia* there came a pause in Miss
Cather's own story. *Youth and the Bright Medusa* is a
kind of intermezzo of hesitancy between prairie land

and Bohemia. Four of the short stories are reprinted from *The Troll Garden* of eight years earlier: a study in the temperament of a city-bred boy whose appetite for beauty and luxury lead him to theft, a week of nectar and ambrosia, and suicide; the overwhelming experience of a concert-lover's first taste of music after a quarter-century of exile in the Far West; the death in the West of a consumptive singer who longs for the thrill and glamour of her finest years; and the already mentioned "Sculptor's Funeral." The three purely exotic stories from the earlier collection were not reprinted. It was the savor of the frontier that Miss Cather chose to preserve. Yet, oddly enough, the four new stories in the later volume have none of this; all but one are devoted to the songstress in prosperity, and except for that one they contribute little to the total achievement of the author.

Evidently Miss Cather was not even yet firmly established in the home of her imagination. She was attached to the prairie stretches and the pioneer types, but only in the half-sentimental fashion of Jim Burden, Antonia's successful friend who had gone out into the world of men and affairs and in his strivings and thrivings looked back with an affectionate sympathy which expressed itself in an occasional hurried visit to the old neighborhood. He had outgrown it, like his youth, and, like his youth, it symbolized to him the "precious, the in-

communicable past.'' In this short-story intermezzo
Miss Cather, sitting in a New York apartment hotel
after a turn around Washington Square, dealt with
the past tenderly and sympathetically, but as one
who was evidently looking back toward it. She did
not actually reawaken it as she had done before.

So it is not surprising that in *One of Ours*, an aftermath of the war, Miss Cather allowed herself to be
warped out of her own orbit, and that as she swung
through space in this flight she oscillated between a
life which she knew to the heart's core and a life of
which she had only a remote and idealized conception. The boy who was "one of ours" belongs to
the same countryside as do Alexandra and Thea and
Antonia. He is disturbed by the same upwellings
and outreachings of spirit, and like his fellow-pio-
neers is vaguely uncomfortable in the narrowness of
the bed that he has not made for himself. A brutal
accident, and gratitude to the woman who nurses
him in his distress, horribly mismate him. The
woman who is flung into his arms has shown her
one pale gleam of warmth while he is prostrate and
helpless. There is nothing in her to respond to ardor
or even affection. She is absorbed in her own chill
righteousness which has been surpassed in literature
only by the centripetal goodness of that most ob-
noxiously virtuous woman, the Lady in *Comus*. Her
final repudiation, in the name of the Lord, of every

wifely duty, sets the boy adrift just as America enters the war. Enlistment seems to offer him the hope of salvation. Fired with the fine zeal which inflamed the first thousands who responded to the call, he sets out on the crusade to save the world for democracy. Stupidity, sordidness, and chicane cannot overcome him. Reminders of the hollowness of his own lot cannot embitter him. In a final white heat of fervor he meets a glorious death on the battlefield.

It is a fine conception, and it is rather thrillingly executed. It may be true of what happened to some of the fallen; and in its heroic consummation it is certainly what those left to mourn would like to believe of every man who fell. Yet the romantic conception of war as a purifying fire belongs to the hopes of the new recruits and to the cherished beliefs of the noncombatant. The truth about warfare has been often rediscovered of late. I have yet to find a soldier who has been long at the front who has read the book without a feeling of revulsion at the concluding chapters. Barbusse and Dos Passos, Remarque and Hemingway, are more likely to be to their taste. The death of Miss Cather's hero has been to them the snuffing of a candle rather than the apotheosis of a lover of democracy.

However far Miss Cather strayed from the paths which she treads with sure foot, when she rambled

into the latter part of *One of Ours*, she was at any
rate not abandoning the theme of all her best work
thus far—the strife for self-fulfilment. Her soldier-
boy-to-be begins his career in the frontier region of
the three heroines. He encounters there the jealous
leveling standards that would reduce all pioneers to
jack-of-all-trade-ship and general undistinction; and
in his army career his restless spirit confronts conditions analogous to those that confront an artist in a
philistine world. But in *A Lost Lady* Miss Cather
lost her bearings altogether. The lost lady lives in
the open West, the only common factor between her
and the heroines of her other novels. Yet the relative distinction of the other women is not that they
live and work where other pioneers do but that
they have in them the stuff of which noble pioneers
and successful artists are made: health, courage, a
desire for freedom, a will to achieve. If they come
through the ordeal their victories are worth win-
ning. If they fail, their failures are tragic because
they have the possibilities of victory in them. But
the lost lady is a weakling and a ne'er-do-well. She
is a tarnished woman whose immorality lies not so
much in the specific infractions of laws and precepts
as in the fact that such a life as hers is inherently
self-defeating. She is not even brilliantly alluring.
Miss Cather has contended that the scarlet woman
is as obsolete as a red-flannel petticoat; but the lost

lady is neither scarlet nor obsolete. The Elizabethans with their sure word usage did well to call such a woman a "drab." Miss Cather's best creative work has been with genuinely creative and colorful people, though this secondary work is a happy illustration of effective narrative technique.

The disruptive influences of the war, disastrous to many a writer who had reached maturity before its outbreak, affected Miss Cather without disastrous results. They are apparent in *The Professor's House* and *My Mortal Enemy;* but as one considers them with the foregoing pair and this quartet with the two that followed, a pattern emerges which is so nicely symmetrical that one at first suspects it, fearful of having fashioned it out of less than sound materials. The early group, up to *My Antonia*, to recapitulate, deals with creative energies in the studio and on the plains, struggling for self-fulfilment and, by grace of their own natures and the assistance of the author, achieving it. After an interval of four years the post-bellum group is concerned with weaker personalities—native Americans subjected to American contemporary life, baffled, frustrated, defeated by it.

Finally *Death Comes for the Archbishop* and *Shadows on the Rock* turn from the Anglo-Saxon, Protestant American scene to the early days of Spanish-American and French Colonial culture and find security in the most substantially enduring tradition in the modern Occident—the authority of the Church of Rome.

It is a cycle with epic implications, which fortunately are left as implications and not advanced as a thesis. It affirms the dramatic past, with its wealth of opportunity for action and for victory. It denies the fruitfulness of contemporary life with its material pressures and its social conservatisms. And it finds repose in a tranquil culture, a life of unity and order, resting on authority and on an established mode of living and believing. "What is any art?" Miss Cather has asked, "but an effort to make a sheath, a mould in which to imprison for a moment the shining, elusive element which is life itself—life hurrying past us and running away, too strong to stop, too sweet to lose?" Miss Cather, more fortunate than most others, has found the satisfactory mould, while many a contemporary is doomed to groping in the realm of chaos and dreadful night.

X

Sinclair Lewis

IN A burst of enthusiasm for John Dos Passos' *Manhattan Transfer* Sinclair Lewis once described his ideal of a novel. It was finer than the novel that inspired him and, as an ideal, finer than any of his own. What he asserted, partly paraphrased and mostly quoted, came to this:

The ideal novel—what may be the foundation of a whole school of fiction—will do what all novelists thus far have failed to do; it will present the panorama, the soul, of a whole community. It will be full of the passion for the beauty and stir of life—of people, and rivers, and little hills, and tall towers by dawn, and furnace-kindled dusk. It will not be sordid, though it will be called so. For even Keats felt no more passionately sensitive a reaction to beauty than will inform it. It will not be literary breakfast food, easy for the moron's digestion; nor in suave couplets, nor in descriptions of skyscrapers so neat that the renters of office space will beg to reprint them. It will deal not in photography but in broken color. It will give the town, smell of it, sound of it, harsh and stirring sight of it; the churn and crunch of littered water between ferry-bow and slip; the midnight of skyscrapers where a dot of yellow will betray an illicit lover or an overworked accountant; insane clamor of subways in the dark; taste of spring in the law-haunted park; shriek of cabaret and groan of loneliness in hall bedrooms; a thousand divinations of beauty without a touch of arty beauty-mongering. Naturally it will be free of the sickly complex which hates the lyrical, charming, demure aspects of beauty, and perversely proclaims ugliness as alone noble, the natural but jejune revolution against the prettifying of the machine-made commercial tale. The writer of such novels will be slated as low and sordid. He will not depict a life that approaches the ideals of a Hartford insurance agent. He will describe it as "a roaring, thundering, incalculable, obscene, magnificent glory."

Mr. Lewis has not written anything of this sort; nor has anyone else; but the direction of his work was for some years an approach toward this, and the thing that he did in *The Job* and *Main Street* and *Babbitt* and *Arrowsmith* served for a while as a promise as well as a performance. Certainly he has for the most part made the community in changing guises serve as his central character.

He began with *Our Mr. Wrenn*, a book as modest and unimpressive as the title character. Mr. Wrenn is a nobody of the business world, faithful, biddable, with a spark of romance which makes him yearn for the grand adventure of travel. A legacy gives him the chance to go to England on a cattle boat, where he tarries uneasily for a few weeks before scurrying back to the big city and his little job. The only thing that happens to him—quite unconvincingly—is that he falls under the spell of an alluring, bohemian dabbler in the arts, and interests her enough to be made the plaything of a little longer than the moment. Then New York again, a new boarding-house, emancipation from a harridan landlady, a meeting with the inevitable "she," a momentary re-encounter with the titian dabbler, and a wrenlike domesticity to which he is happily resigned as he hurries home beneath a sunset which no longer lures him to stray, with seven cents' worth of potato salad and the prospect of the evening paper and a game of pinochle with Nellie.

The Trail of the Hawk, another youthful book, is much more vigorous, introducing several who were to reappear in other novels with new names. Carl Ericson has the makings of Martin Arrowsmith. His Ruth is a forerunner of Joyce Lanyon. Bone Stillman, village atheist, is a pre-incarnation of Miles Bjornstam. It is the tale of a stormy petrel rather than a hawk, who marries, as Mr. Lewis liked to marry his men, a lady who cares more for the amenities than he does, but more for him than for the amenities. It tells of their love-makings and tiffs and reconciliations and in the last chapter sends them to sea on an indeterminate vagabondage, he quoting Kipling and she speculating on the possibility of a Society for the Spread of Madness among the Respectable. On the whole it is a rather engaging novel. It is built around a real character with some slight capacities to roar and thunder, with a tinge of the hobo, a strain of virginity, a flair for adventure, and a hanker for taking risks; one of the type who by the hundreds were soon to flock to the first officers' training camps and to find themselves, for a while at least, in a life which was measured by something more challenging than a time-clock routine. As a social chameleon Carl is a little out of character, for he is quick as a girl in taking on the protective coloration, when he does not forget himself, of the best people; and he develops what collegians of his day called a "line" of pseudo-clever talk, which his author seems to enjoy as much as he does though it could hardly intrigue anybody but post-adolescent readers. More significant than this is the bromidic conversation of secondary characters which was to figure so largely in later stories.

With two books behind him Mr. Lewis did not hurry. It was two years later when *The Job* appeared, presenting the city at closer range and more nearly as his ideal novelist would present it. During

these two years Mr. Lewis' mind became—in the
slang phrase of pedagogy—socialized. He had discovered what pedagoguese would term two phe-
nomena—the Social Order and Woman-in-Business.
Una Golden, without knowing it at the start, is a
modernist. She has seen through the futility of the
male sex in terms of her father and her elderly suitor
of Panama, Pennsylvania. She advances on Manhattan, learns typewriting and stenography, gets one
position after another, finds out about the drabness
and pettiness of the business system and, for a moment, the almost beautiful thing that business can
be. She marries a bounder, is eventually freed from
him, starts anew, develops an ability to plan and to
perform, creates a real job of her own, and then re-
joins the one man who has ever deeply appealed to
her. It is a novel with a solution; for the Woman-
in-Business comes into her own when life permits
her to retain her job and gives her a baby to boot;
but the idiom is an unhappy one, and the story ends
too soon. More exactly, life promises her a baby to
neglect.

The Job is more convincing than the two novels
that preceded it and, for that matter, than the two
negligible stories that followed: *The Innocents* and
Free Air. Mr. Lewis is not primarily a story-teller;
he is an expositor who uses the narrative form. To
follow an individual through his experiences as one

would follow and observe a force in nature, to see him always as an individual and yet to see in him the human elements which are timeless—that is neither his interest nor his gift. To Mr. Lewis a story if it has any vitality must serve not merely as a story but also as a vehicle. Life for him is not inherent in John Smith or in George Babbitt; it is the force that surrounds the man. In applauding Dos Passos he applauded him not for creating character but for painting the panorama of the metropolis. Of Zenith, the middle-sized city, he has written, "Vast is the power of cities to reclaim the wanderer. More than mountains or the shore-devouring sea, a city retains its character, imperturbable, cynical, holding behind apparent changes its essential purpose." It is small wonder that with this in mind he has with a single exception never made characters strong enough to dominate the stories of which they have been only incidental features. Una Golden is not this character. She is singularly colorless even in her success, though as a type she is significant as one of an endless procession of women marching down the Main Streets, expressing their discontent with life as they find it, and vaguely asserting their right to make something vaguely different from it. The city is in this book, and an idea is in it, and, more important than these, satire for the first time asserts itself effectively. Lewis has arrived at his own manner when, for example, he writes of Pemberton's, "It has been calculated that ninety-three million women in all parts of the world have ruined their complexions, and therefore their souls, by Pemberton's creams and lotions for saving the same; and that nearly three-tenths of the alcohol consumed in prohibition counties is obtained in Pemberton's tonics and blood-builders and women's specifics, these last being regarded by large farmers with beards as especially tasty and stimulating. Mr. Pemberton is the Napoleon of patent medicine, and also the Napoleon of drugs used by physicians to cure the effects of patent medicines. He is the Shakespeare of ice-cream sodas, and the Edison of hot-water bags."

If the account were to move in perfect order, the next step to record would be Mr. Lewis' advance on the city. But his next attempt in fact was to picture the heart and mind of America. Wiseacres had been saying for a generation that the time had passed for the writing of the American novel; that America was too far flung and heterogeneous for any such possible document. They had been saying it because they could not imagine a story that might include Tom Sawyer and Posson Jone and Uncle Remus and Colonel Carter and Silas Lapham and Rose of Dutcher's Coolly and William Sylvanus Baxter in the same company. No such company could be imagined outside of fantasy. They lived too early. But a few ingenious men changed all that by the extensive use of wires and rails and gasoline and billboards.

There had been two literary—more or less literary —traditions of the American small town. One was, as Mr. Lewis reminded us, "the one sure abode of friendship, honesty and clean-sweet marriageable girls." In story after story the American youth made his pilgrimage, had his fling, renounced the world and the sins of the metropolis, and returned to the village street, the white picket fence, the faithful family dog, the lilacs, the moonlight, an armful of innocence, and happiness ever after It was Auburn, loveliest village of the plain, but it was not America. The other tradition was that villages were chiefly featured by "whiskers, iron dogs upon lawns, gold-bricks, checkers, jars of gilded cat-tails, and shrewd, comic old men who are known as 'hicks' and who ejaculate 'Waal, I swan!' " This village too had disappeared in the days of Silas Lapham and Colonel Carter.

The climax of civilization, said Lewis, was the town that "thinks not in hoss-swapping, but in cheap motor-cars, telephones, ready-made clothes, silos, alfalfa, phonographs, leather-upholstered Morris chairs, bridge prizes, oil stocks, motion-pictures, land deals, unread sets of Mark Twain, and a chaste version of national politics." This provincial town with its standardization of mediocrity might be let alone, he thought, if it were merely passive; but "it has become a force seeking to dominate the earth, to drain the hills and the sea of color. . . . . Its conception of a community ideal is not the grand manner, the noble aspiration, the fine aristocratic pride, but cheap labor for the kitchen and rapid increase in the price of land. . . . . If all the provincials were kindly there would be no reason for desiring the town to seek great traditions. It is the small, busy men, crushingly powerful in their common purpose, viewing themselves as men of the world but keeping themselves men of the cash-register and the comic film, who make the town a sterile oligarchy"; attempting to subject the entire country to the domination of the fundamentalists, prohibitionists, 100 per cent Americans, and go-getters.

As a thesis and an indictment this is clear enough, and it is based on plenty of evidence. It is not only sound in general but it is reasonable in particular, as it takes issue with the kind of standardization that results in obnoxious stupidity in contrast with the passive kindliness which may be stupid but which is for the most part harmless. Excellence in a thesis novel, however, requires excellence in the novel as well as in the thesis; and it requires incomparably good story-telling to carry the double pack. Lewis admits great admiration for Dickens, who could carry both burdens, and praises him, as who does not, for his creation of characters but condemns him for dragging in pages of "lying hypocrisy." Lewis neither achieves nor offends with Dickens. *Main Street* pretty largely makes its case as a case but leaves in the memory no unforgettable episode and no imperative person. One comes with a touch of surprise to a passage which alludes to Champ Perry and Sam Clark as kindly and to Harry Haydock, Dave Dyer, and Jackson Elder as the malignants in the social group. A review of the text shows that the author is right, but without the reminder and the checkup they all merge into one indistinguishably vulgar and stupid crowd. The few whom one remembers are not essentially Main Streeters. Carol Kennicott is the Woman-out-of-Business, a foil and complement to Una Golden. Doc Kennicott perhaps represents Gopher Prairie, but in the story he is used only to play up to the leading lady, though he is bigger than his role. One has vague memories of others but cannot recall their names.

Mr. Lewis did, of course, create a character in George F. Babbitt; and his success as an artistic creation lies in the fact that he is not the caricature that he is usually said to be. He is sufficiently complicated to belong to the race of little people who are often more multiplex than the great ones of the earth, whose greatness lies in their relative simplicity. And his defeat as an individual arises from the fact that he actually struggles to extricate himself from the web of circumstance which is too close for him but to which he never completely surrenders. He plans to become a lawyer until he finds a trusting brown head on his shoulder which considers itself engaged to him. Lacking the brutality to disillusion it, he makes money in real estate. He inclines toward honesty, but an astute and unscrupulous senior partner involves him in transactions which, lacking belligerence, he winks at. He wants to be faithful to his perfunctory marriage vows, but he is bored into a shuffling intrigue with an alluring client. He would like to be something more than a timidly abusive standpatter, but, in the face of the gang of good fellows whose approval is the light of day to him, he is afraid to pay the price of social and business ostracism.

Always around him, overwhelming all but the last vestige of protest in him, is the city, a city of the potential splendors and roarings and thunderings that Mr. Lewis has never yet pictured. It reclaims Babbitt and standardizes him. The material side of it he likes; he flutters feebly against the regimentation of thought. And in the end, irredeemably Babbitt, he still yearns that his son may have better luck: "I've never done a single thing that I wanted to in my whole life! I don't know's I've accomplished anything except just get along. I figure out I've made about a quarter of an inch out of a possible hundred rods. Well, maybe you'll carry on things further. I don't know. But I do get a kind of sneaking pleasure out of the fact that you knew what you wanted to do, and did it. Well, these folks in there will try to bully you, and tame you down. Tell 'em to go to the devil. I'll back you. Take your factory job if you want to. Don't be scared of the family. No, nor of all Zenith. Nor of yourself, the way I've been." Lewis might have adopted "The Custom of the Country," as a title, as Mrs. Wharton once did; but *Babbitt* is better for this book, which has to do with an indubitable character. In a measure it is true that Babbitt rode to fame down Main Street; but a populous street never yet gave more than the opportunity for an imposing procession, and Babbitt's progress was at the head of an innumerable army.

Lewis' reputation was established on these two novels; but so, too, was a pattern of writing for him. Martin Arrowsmith was the next to be offered as a sacrifice on the altar of public mediocrity.

He stands at a far intellectual pole from Babbitt, but he has a similar history, and, granting the superiority of his native gifts, he comes off very little better. One conventional story of the period has dealt with the young genius who grows up in uncongenial surroundings, stifled now by poverty, now by Mammon, now by dilettantism. Then he achieves as an artist and enjoys the satisfaction of turning up his nose at the world as he espouses poverty or marries wealth. Arrowsmith is a genius, but a scientist. He has a conception of science which sets it on the plane with art and religion. It makes a man uncontent with half-knowledge. The business game is a silly insufficiency to him; so is the unfounded pursuit of dreamy idealism. He is an intolerant worker for human welfare with slight respect for most human beings. He does not expect intelligent sympathy, and he is ready to make sacrifices. "In Martin Arrowsmith there were no decorative heroisms, no genius for amours, no exotic wit, no edifyingly borne misfortunes. He presented neither picturesque elegance nor a moral message. He was full of hasty faults and of a perverse honesty; a young man, often unkindly, often impolite. But he had one gift, a curiosity whereby he saw nothing as ordinary."

He is human enough, then, to be put into a story —the story of the scientist in conflict with his avowed allies. An old bacteriologist fills him with apostolic zeal which wanes before the need of supporting a wife. For a while he is a Will Kennicott, a by no means despicable country doctor. Then he becomes a health department official in a western town where boosting for better babies is encouraged as long as the milk supply is let alone. The pictures of village and town life are convincing, and there is an almost Dickensian finality in Almus Pickerbaugh, medical demagogue and ultimate congressman. Then Lewis and Arrowsmith together invade New York City, and the same thing happens to them that happens to the young crusader when he first fell in with preventive medicine: "Everything became clear to Martin—too clear."

These two young men descend on the metropolis armed with a deadly thesis. They are to demonstrate that though the countryside is inhospitable to the fine enthusiasms of the scientist, the great city is more dangerous. It offers the scientific investigator a laboratory and assistance and a living wage, but it begrudges him the time to follow his curiosity to its final goal, to be certain of his findings, to be deliberate and modest in the statement of his conclusions. The country is stupid, but the city is subtly and insidiously demoralizing. According to this thesis, control of the great research foundations inevitably falls into the hands of exploiters and publicity seekers. To yield to them is to compromise with the devil. To oppose them is not merely to risk personal success but to put in jeopardy the fine ends to which the scientist is dedicated. To take up with the fashionable patrons of good works is to enter the purgatory especially devised for the objects of polite patronage. A genuine devotee of the truth in such a dilemma is doomed to be either broken or banished.

This is a striking proposition based on a deal of philistinism in the medical world. Some of the originals of his character studies are recognizable; the rest, with the exception of Tubbs the exploiter, are well above the level of caricature. But the story falters in two respects. The lesser is the result of attempting to put unfamiliar and technical material into a story fable. Lewis was weak on scientific procedure just as later he was to be on ecclesiastical thought and polity. The major weakness arises from his overinsistence on the thesis. Telling a partial truth about the medical world, he implies that it is a universal truth. The research scientist is not an inevitable victim. Pasteur, facing every obstacle, fought the French to a finish and won. Many an American man in medical research has not compounded with principle and has been a free agent in a full career with abounding honors. There is no hint of such a figure in the fable; and Arrowsmith's retreat to solitary activity is recorded as inevitable, not only to his nature, but also to the nature of the case. It was inevitable for him only because he was an unheroic figure. Yet he was developed as a third witness against the baleful stupidity of the American public.

Mr. Lewis was now in high career as a special state's attorney intent on making a reputation by piling up convictions. His next witness is not the frustrated idealist but the successful exploiter. Elmer Gantry, whose name is also a book-title, is a rogue and a bounder who chooses the ministry for his calling because he is bred for it, evangelized into it, and finds in it an outlet for part of his emotions and all his instinct for exhibitionism. Ousted from his first Baptist pulpit, but not unfrocked, he does well in commercial salesmanship until he falls under the spell of a woman evangelist, and as her assistant and devotee he comes nearest to decency. In fact, she is so commanding a figure that the author had to invoke a holocaust to get her out of the story—an obvious and desperate device, for Gantry's soul was not to be saved, and he was in imminent peril of salvation. After an adventure in New Thought in which he pilfers from his prophetess and is discharged, he finds an opening in Methodism in which he progresses through increasingly remunerative pastorates, irredeemably corrupt and headed toward a bishopric as the story ends.

Elmer Gantry is in one phase Mr. Lewis' first attempt at a rake's progress, the point of which, as a narrative genre, is that the rake is not unique but a typical product of the social order. His progress is by way of a series of intrigues, all but one of them shabby: with Juanita, the daughter of a neighboring farmer, a willing choir singer, a chambermaid at Solomon Junction, Lulu Bains, Sharon Falconer, Lulu again, a Chautauqua "talent," and finally with an adventuress who in order to save her own skin refrains from ruining him by public exposure. He has a punch which he resorts to against three successive hecklers at meetings interspersed along his career and against a spindling bootlegger on a sensational raid. And in his own parlance he has a "punch" in the pulpit which depends on the same physique and voice and abounding energy which intrigue women and win him an election to the Rotary Club.

He was a timely figure in 1927, and in his timeliness he achieved a smashing *succés de scandal;* but timeliness made the book a contribution to journalism rather than to literature. Like Martin Arrowsmith, Gantry was proponent for a thesis which the author was acquainted with through investigation and case study rather than through experience and unconscious observation. Lewis was involved in trying at one time to tell a story, build a character, indict the public, and deal with material for which he had no intimate feeling. He apparently recognized the failure of the narrative to carry its own burden and confessed it by the interpolation of long and dispensable dialogues which were relevant to the thesis but not to the plot, because they are carried on between decent and intelligent parsons to whom the priestly rogue is alien in manners, morals, and mind.

With the publication of *Elmer Gantry* Sinclair Lewis was just entering middle life and presumably was in mid-career; but since then he has written only two books of moment, one dwelling on the potentialities of the American type and one on the possibility of a democratic debacle. One was his best novel and the most popular—in print, on the stage, and on the screen—since *Main Street;* the other, his most striking propagandist piece, a satirical extravaganza.

After all the Jeremiads that he poured out so insistently and at last so tediously, he turned to the other side of the medal, concluding wisely that he had not told the whole story; that life, particularly the life of a region or an era, is never all of one tone, cannot be disposed of in one formula. In evidence of which he wrote *Dodsworth*. Life in a new country, he recalled at last, demands fortitude, which may be great enough not only to survive but also to do the work exacted of it. Now and again an idealist survives the harsh experience; beats nature at its own game and stays blithe; holds his own in the free-for-all without becoming money-mad; keeps his head and maintains his own sense of values in spite of the safe and sane and the returners to normalcy. So Lewis presented in Sam Dodsworth a man strong enough first to succeed and then to withstand success; who retires from fortune-making, travels, and coming home resolves to invest his wealth and his energy in his own way of doing what he thinks is worth doing. He does not buy himself off by endowing a college, a museum, or an orchestra, but goes back to making automobiles—a new sort that people can enjoy going slow in; and he dreams of building beautiful suburbs, authentically American, far from the crazy agglomerations of architectural odds and ends that surround most of our cities today.

The significance of *Dodsworth* is that instead of representing just the energy of the frontiersman put to work toward ends that he has never dreamed of and instead of admiring an insatiable desire for activity as an end in itself, Lewis makes of this big cub a dreamer who at fifty decides to continue his education, to find out what he is involved in, and to keep on dreaming. He is a Babbitt undefeated, an

Arrowsmith with a backbone, for he is big enough to withstand the silly coerciveness of men who are littler than he and to learn from men who are bigger. So when Elon Richards, cosmopolite and financial magnate, advises him after his retirement to return to the American adventure, "because it is an adventure that we have here—the greatest in the world—and not a certainty of manners in an uncertainty of the future, like all of Europe," he assents. Richards, he concludes, is right. "Our adventure is going to be the bigger because we do feel that Europe has a lot we need. We're no longer satisfied with the log cabin and the corn pone. We want everything that Europe has. We'll take it." Dodsworth has graduated from the school that could mistake the "everything" of Richards' remark for material belongings. He admits his inexperience and sets about to learn from the past and to keep on growing in wisdom as well as in stature.

In his admiring commentary on Dos Passos, Lewis wrote on the assumption that truth should be conveyed implicitly in the novel, without exposition from the author. The ideal novel would not be easy to understand; in its faithfulness to life it would be incalculable. In the major tales which earned him his fame Mr. Lewis in a measure lived up to this assumption; but in turning away from these three criticisms of life he either documented, argued, and harangued or, as in such negligible books as *Mantrap*, *Work of Art*, and *The Prodigal Parents*, he was merely going through the motions of writing a novel. *It Can't Happen Here* is stirring, but it is a nightmare projected against the American scene. As time has passed Mr. Lewis has progressively surrendered to what he called "the sickly complex whereby one hates the lyrical . . . . and perversely proclaims ugliness." In theory and practice he once showed that he was capable of more than this, but in effect there seems to have been less of Sam Dodsworth in him than of Martin Arrowsmith, and like the latter he has been unfaithful to his high calling.

XI
John Dos Passos

THE special object of these chapters is to observe the use of American materials by American novelists. Most of the writers have been identifiable with regions. Sinclair Lewis, however, has ranged from Minnesota to Florida and New York, with a unifying element of the Main Street or Middletown concept of life which he attributes to the United States as a whole. Thomas Wolfe, rural southerner, translated into metropolitan northerner, and betimes homesick traveler, was concerned with the "unquiet heart, the vast incertitude, the huge sprawled wealth" of the land which he loved in spite of himself. Willa Cather has ventured widely. And Dos Passos in his most ambitious venture, the trilogy, *U.S.A.*, once undertook more systematically than any other to represent a money-mad democracy in which the predatory instinct, now dominant, may be first controlled and then perhaps transformed into something less primitive, more benevolent.

This is a simple formula; but an estimate of Dos Passos may not be simple because of two complicating factors: first, that the man himself represents an unresolved dilemma, and, second, that he has provided a battleground for critics as to both his viewpoint and his technique. To stick to the special object therefore demands attention to what he has written about, his subject matter, his America; and to avoid ignoring questions at issue calls for at least brief comment on the ways he has written, his technique, and on his point of view, the essential man.

As to the objective scenes, persons, and places in Dos Passos' novels, *One Man's Initiation* (a title which might apply to the writer as well as to his central character, a negligible figment) resembles his mature works only in that the scene is predominantly urban and that, as in *Streets of Night*, the people are urban nonconformists who are clearer about what they dissent from than about what they believe. These novels are as unreal and as unnatural as the early tales of Stephen Crane and Upton Sinclair. We can let them go at that. In the far more substantial *Three Soldiers*, which appeared between them, urban characters and philosophy predominate also, derived as they are from the backgrounds of two of the trio and from most of the other Americans in their overseas experience. There is also a suggestion of the coming panoramic effects in the interwoven histories of three boys so different as Fuseli, Californian immigrant, Christfield, quintessence of Indiana, and Andrews, Virginian-Harvard musician.

Somewhat deviously these three books lead toward *Manhattan Transfer*, which, like the following trilogy, is pre-eminently an effort to picture not characters or plot but a cross-section of American metropolitan life. It was of this volume that Sinclair Lewis wrote with such gusto the comments I have already paraphrased (p. 164) which will bear re-reading at this point; but another passage is peculiarly relevant at the moment, for the purpose of Dos Passos is fractionally like that of his great predecessor. It is a bit from the author's introduction to the *Comédie Humaine*.

"It was no small task," Balzac wrote, "to depict the two or three thousand conspicuous types of a period. . . . . This crowd of actors, of characters, this multitude of lives, needed a setting—if I may be pardoned the expression, a gallery. Hence the very natural division into scenes of Private Life, of Provincial Life, of Parisian, Political, Military and Country Life. . . . . The scenes of Private Life represent childhood and youth and their errors, as the scenes of Provincial Life represent the age of passion, scheming, self-interest and ambition. Then the scenes of Parisian Life give a picture of the tastes and vices and unbridled powers which conduce to the habits peculiar to great cities, where the extremes of good and evil meet." Substitute "Manhattan" for "Parisian" and you will be prepared for the "tastes and vices and unbridled power" which are peculiar to Dos Passos' novel of metropolitan life.

Manhattan Transfer cannot be epitomized. Two characters are more persistently recurrent than any others. Ellen Thatcher, daughter of a bookkeeper, seeps up through the lower levels of the show business, marries and is divorced from a degenerate third-rate actor, falls in love with a rich young ne'er-do-weel and has a child by him, allures and resists a theatrical producer, accepts the protection of marriage with a newspaper man but does not give him either her love or her body, and at the end of the book is world-wearily drifting on to new but stale experiences with other men. Jimmy Herf enters the book in the first cabin of an Atlantic liner, becomes an orphan, gets enough education to go into newspaper work, loathes it but sticks to it, and among all the heterogeny of New York becomes a pal of the young ne'er-do-weel and a protector of the young actress. At the end, bereft of one by his death and of the other by her indifference, he leaves town jobless and penniless, starts hitch-hiking, and when asked how far he is going, supplies the book with

its concluding words: "I dunno. . . . . Pretty far."
Yet these comments give a false impression of an
organized tale. Jimmy and Ellen are only two out
of scores who are presented in disjunctive episodes
of a few pages each, some of them disappearing
without being dismissed, most of them recurrent
and loosely connected either by definite contacts
and relationships or by being parts of a huge, unpat-
terned fabric. The total impression is of a vast, hectic, sordid welter of getters and spenders. Now and
again there is the suggestion of a social theory, but
it is, like all the other elements in the book, hinted
at and dropped, possibly to recur from some other
character in some other connection, comparable to
scraps of dialogue heard in passing on a crowded
Broadway pavement.

In his foreword to *U.S.A.*, Dos Passos suggests
what he wants to do or what he has tried to do. A
country boy, like the boy at the opening of *Manhattan Transfer*, is in town wanting a job and thinking of country jobs—road-mending, fishing, bridge-
tending, dirt-farming, driving a locomotive. He
sees the emptying streets at the end of a work day
and, in his mind's eye, he glimpses far reaches of the
land over which he has wandered from the West to
the Gulf and the Great Lakes and on to a training
camp in the East. (This is in the mood of Whitman.) Then he hears America (and this is in the

mood of Sandburg): "In his mother's words telling about longago, in his father's telling about when I was a boy, in the kidding stories of uncles, in the lies the kids told at school, the hired man's yarns, the tall tales the doughboys told after taps;

"It was the speech that clung to the ears, the link that tingled in the blood; U.S.A.

"U.S.A. is the slice of a continent. U.S.A. is a group of holding companies, some aggregations of trade unions, a set of laws bound in calf, a radio network, a chain of moving picture theatres, a column of stock quotations rubbed out and written in by a Western Union boy on a blackboard, a publiclibrary full of old newspapers and dogeared historybooks with protests scrawled on the margins in pencil. . . . . U.S.A. is the letters at the end of an address when you are away from home. But mostly U.S.A. is the speech of the people."

In the trilogy—The *42d Parallel* (1930), *Nineteen-nineteen* (1932), and *The Big Money* (1936)—Dos Passos represents the country through two sets of characters: the fictitious, who carry the narratives and speak in their own persons, and the actual historical figures, who embody the moving forces behind American life and whose word portraits are in the nervous, staccato, American speech of the author.

The fictive characters are egocentric, with no constant theory of life beyond getting along on or against the current; and most of them end by drifting with it. All told, there are scores of them; but a dozen are featured by the sections entitled for them. Four of these see life through the eyes of the downtrodden: Fainy McCreary, who vacillates between fighting for the hard-pressed and taking life easy; Joe Williams, who spends his years on the sea, cruising, carousing, drifting; Ben Compton, who enlists in the ranks of aggressive labor and is both sent to federal prison and expelled from the ranks of the Communist party as the double price of his individualism; and Mary French, a college girl of markedly mixed parentage, frivolous and serious, who surrenders spirit, mind, and body to the communist-labor group and gains only in what she gives.

Four of the twelve who carry title roles are aesthete bohemians: Eleanor Stoddard, who is selfish enough to keep her balance and be miserably successful in her little wire-pulling, cocktail-drinking world; Eveline Hutchins, her spineless counterpart, whose fate in the House of Mirth is as abysmal as that of Mrs. Wharton's Lily Bart; Dick Savage and Ann Elizabeth Trent, male and female, variations on the same theme. A final quartet among the preferred dozen in the long Dos Passos roster ride high in the money-mad world he pictures: Margo Dowling, stepchild of the theater and a show-girl adventuress, is a development in her shabby success of the earlier Ellen Thatcher Oglethorpe Herf; Jane Williams, sister of Joe the sailor, is high only by being the tail of a kite, private secretary to J. Ward Moorehouse, the immensely platitudinous and immensely successful public relations council; and, finally, Charley Anderson, Dakota machinist and airplane engineer, who arrives in history in time to exploit and be exploited until, after his daily experience of drinking too much, he drives his automobile just not fast enough to pass a railroad crossing ahead of an express train. There they are, the leading types depicted by the American Balzac, representative of the multitude of others, hectic and purposeless, as much of American life was in the first quarter of the century, the flotsam and jetsam of a turbulent period.

In this almost exclusively metropolitan world of *Manhattan Transfer* and *U.S.A.* the inhabitants give full license to the "tastes and vices and unbridled powers which conduce to the habits peculiar to great cities." This, if he should choose to cite it, is eminent authority for Dos Passos' recital; but if he should cite it he should also cite in the quotation what he has not included in his novels: "where the extremes of good and evil meet." (Balzac listed more than thirty "virtuous persons" of major and minor importance in his works.) However, the city supplies the examples for Dos Passos, though Howells and James and Mrs. Wharton found characters who seemed more normal to them and for whom the city also supplied examples. Furthermore, these others in different degrees indicated or implied the kinds of behavior and misbehavior on which Dos Passos dwells reiteratively to the last syllable of speech and action. He dilates, one might say, on the New Year's Eve celebrants who drink and drink and drink yet more, and talk loud and shout and scream, and stumble off to beds in which they find next morning whom they have slept with; while the more conventional novelists described people who talked and laughed and had their mild potations and then went home with their husbands or wives. The city contains both kinds, and both know what life is, for it is mistaken to presume that life is only license. Yet it is difficult to find any other presumption in Dos Passos. I read at random thirty pages from *Nineteen-nineteen*, and on more than half are references or descriptions to excessive drinking; I read thirty other pages, and on more than two-thirds there is promiscuous sex intercourse. Drinking is sometimes checked by lack of funds, but there is no apparent bar to copulation. Dos Passos reveals no inclination to characterize men and women and to keep the characterization alive except by exact transcription. Waiving the question of propriety, one may still raise the question of taste, and if one concede for the sake of the argument—which I do not—even the question of taste, one may plead that the repetition is wearisome. A child repeats twenty, thirty times; a normal adult recognizes that if he has not made himself understood to adults at the third or fourth assertion, he may as well give up the attempt.

It is a commonplace that, as the basic assumptions behind private and public life have shifted or been shaken in the present era, the assumptions of the more sensitive novelists have shifted as to how fictional people will behave and how their behavior will be judged by enlightened readers. H. G. Wells's *Experiment in Autobiography* shows how far ahead of his time he was in enunciating a theory. It was the modern temper in the man that made it hard for him to communicate with his sister, whose "world was like an interior by a Dutch master" while her brother's was a "loose, headlong panorama of all science, history and literature." This Wellsian temper baffled Henry James, an unwilling but fascinated victim of the author, who declared that he was unable and unwilling to approach or take leave of the novels "in any projected light of criticism, in any judging or concluding, any comparing, in fact in any aesthetic or 'literary' relation at all. . . . ." It baffled James because the novel had for generations been founded on a reliance in social fixity, a frame of reference, and now the "splintering frame had begun to get into the picture."

This leads us to the nonfictional people who loom large in *U.S.A.* Dos Passos' attempt once more to construct a frame, though a frame reconstructed from splinters, led to the threefold interpolated features: the elusive Camera Eye, the more intelligible Newsreel, and the most effective pen portraits, for which he has supplied no catch-title. In offering a backdrop for his players he could not proceed from any fixity of generalized judgments, but he could proceed from quite the opposite—a varied recital of evidences that generalized judgments do not prevail in American life, that in whole areas personal morality is neither practiced nor appealed to, and that property and proprietorship, in whole areas, are viewed with the callous disregard for public morals which one disclosure after another has demonstrated during the 1930's. With his other discards Dos Passos, along with many a contemporary, has also discarded the attempt to set life in order. Presenting it as he has seen it, he has presented confusion—sometimes worse confounded.

The actual, documentable characters, then, are used as parts of an elaborate frame for the pictorial view of the United States of America. The men and women in this historical collection include leftists of different sorts—Eugene Debs, to start the whole series, Bill Haywood, La Follette, Sr., Jack Reed, Paxton Hibben, Randolph Bourne, Thorstein Veblen; creative geniuses, such as Burbank, Edison, Steinmetz, the Wright brothers in aeronautics and Frank Lloyd Wright in architecture; political leaders like W. J. Bryan, Theodore Roosevelt, and Woodrow Wilson; fortune-makers—Myron Keith, Carnegie, Morgan, Ford, Hearst, Insull. They are introduced not in this order but in relation to the movement of the narrative. In witness, the second book of the trilogy offers as its last two portraits Wesley Everest, lumberjack and ex-doughboy, who was lynched as a striker one Armistice Day, and the Unknown Soldier; the third book presents, just after Veblen, the popular idols, Isadora Duncan and Rudolph Valentino, and ends with the disappearance into the west of a hungry, hitch-hiking vagabond, the two volumes concluding on the same minor key. These are all products of American life. Most are more articulate and more purposeful than the fictional characters, and most can be measured by what society does for the highly conventional and the highly individual. In sum they amount to a satire, conscious or unconscious in its application, on the rewards for the Puritan virtues of industry, thrift, and orthodoxy. Those who practice them go to heaven; their violators are punished with hell, not hereafter but on earth.

Unhappily for *U.S.A.* as a whole, the frame Dos Passos has made is much too fine for the picture. The set of medallions surrounding the stories renders the imagined people pallid and unreal. The literary effect is far higher not because the author has taken more pains with the style but because the subjects have generated a superior style. The historical figures are vivid products of their time. They have driving purposes, and they either succeed spectacularly or go down to spectacular defeat. Their qualities are positive, including not only a capacity for enjoyment but also an actual zest for life. Moreover, their pleasures are not confined to the senses; sex and alcohol play no part in their life-stories as Dos Passos tells them—or only the most fleetingly incidental in one or two—for the things that engross them are dreams and making dreams come true. The projects and the campaigns to achieve them are usually fierce, and they are undistracted by touch and taste and odor. On the contrary, the fictional people live on the plane of the senses, rise now and then only to sink the lower, start with discontent, find relief in feverish pleasure-hunting, fail in all their high objectives, and share in the disintegrating history of the times. The one answer needed to the question whether they fairly represent America is supplied by their creator in the biographic sketches. If Dos Passos offered these to the reader as antidotes he should have made his intention clearer. Neither he nor any friendly critic seems to have explicitly suggested this. But if he did not want them to serve this purpose, he has partially refuted his main theme and blurred the total effect of the trilogy. The U.S.A. is not an ideal land according to either picture or frame; but it is a healthy place according to the frame. The living people breathe ozone instead of carbon dioxide; they thrive on conflict instead of sinking in exhaustion and decay.

In *Adventures of a Young Man* Dos Passos uses similar material and tells a parallel story; but he simplifies his method. There is an order about the narrative, a more conventional procedure in telling it, and a clearer implication that no good end is being gained by the dominant group of unschooled and undisciplined revolutionists. Glenn Spotswood, son of a former Columbia professor who long ago lost his post because of his leftist views, finds out for himself that radicalism, or even liberalism, does not pay, getting his first lesson as counselor in a boys' camp, his second when he takes a short-lived job under a prosperous uncle in a Texas bank, and many a harsher one thereafter. In the meantime sympathetic friends prove to be libertines as well as libertarians, and, though he sees nothing in this to outrage his taste or morals, he sees nothing to convince him that they are effective members of society. Trying to be effective himself, he takes up the cause of the miners, as Ben Compton and Mary French did in *The Big Money*. Here he encounters the paralysis of will resulting from distrust and suspicion among the radicals and from the rigors of Communist party control. Once more he sees social oppression and fascist violence at work but finds that he can fight for freedom in his present alliance only by surrendering all freedom of judgment, will, and action. He goes to Spain as a defender of democracy, as John Andrews of *Three Soldiers* went to France, and in a new subjection of self to the cause of liberty he is cold-bloodedly sent to his death by fellow-revolutionists who select this method of "liquidating" him. I present the outline partly to give an idea of the drift of the novel but also partly because it can be done and done more easily than with any but Dos Passos' earliest works. For the time being he is through with the complex description of complexity, through with standing on a corner in Times Square and reporting life as it surges by. He takes a course of his own choosing.

In style, Dos Passos reaches the peak of effectiveness when he releases the poet and romanticist in himself, as he does in his miniatures. But in the body of his works he insists on holding a stiff rein over Pegasus, forcing him to plod over cobblestones or through muck and mire. The writing is not merely prosaic; it has the dull undistinction of average American speech, not the tang and vividness of American colloquialism that give it a quality of its own. It produces the impression not of having been adopted as a common idiom but of having sunk to that level. When the characters break into dialogue there is a lack of variety again. They all talk pretty much alike with a common shoddiness of speech. Often, moreover, Dos Passos frankly abandons the dialogue form of conversation or discussion and offers a drab summary of successive speeches that might serve as extended notes for a finished passage. "Life is so dull," he seems to say, "and talk is so dull, and I am so bored by it, that I have no heart to reproduce or simulate it. I'll just give you a rough idea of the general drift." The writing is seldom as slovenly as much of Dreiser's, but this seems to be because Dos Passos cannot write quite as badly even when he is quite as careless. And yet in another way he reminds one of Cabell's self-conscious mannerisms—by the inverted preciosity of his conjoined, unhyphenated words. They do not appear to be put together according to any principle, and they accomplish little beyond frequently offering the reader slight optical puzzles in their resistance to interpretation at first glance. For example: thingauze, mortgageridden, peachorchard, fireengine, teathings, billoffare, antisepticlooking. The only reasonable explanation, which is less than justification, for all these blurred and blurring effects is (to cite it once again) the phrase of Hergesheimer that they are signs of a "confusion of forms very like the age." There can be no doubt of their deliberate adoption, even though they seem casually accidental; for Dos Passos' command of good prose is beyond debate.

Dos Passos was for some years acclaimed by the proletarian writers as their leading proponent for the workers, expositor of the class conflict. He and they now enjoy the distant bowing acquaintance of estranged friends. Yet, judging from his novels alone, it is not clear that he ever used them to wave the Marxian banner. He was surely, and is surely, concerned with the effects of industrialism on modern life, though not so surely committed to a corrective program. The Marxian, we are told, accepts industry but rejects private ownership of property. Dos Passos seems to be disturbed by the entire machine age, inclined to deplore its total effects. And he describes the class conflict with mixed feelings, sympathetic to the rank and file, but skeptical of leaders and leadership. In this American economic scene as he represents it, the reader is first made aware of vague conditions which embrace the privileged who are all impoverished in spirit and the underprivileged who are also poor in opportunity and possessions. Behind these conditions is a malignant system and a class cleavage. The most privileged, like George Apley and his friends, realize that they own America and want no change in the conditions which gave it to them. Lawmakers and business executives must see to that. The businessmen as they descend in the scale join with the constabulary in using tactics of which the rich and refined know nothing and cherish their ignorance. These are the tactics from which the underprivileged suffer. Faced by conditions, they formulate a theory in the hope of achieving a change. But in *U.S.A.* and *Adventures of a Young Man* Dos Passos presents the radical counterparts of George Apley in the Marxian theorists who are more solicitous to maintain party solidarity than to rescue definite sufferers from definite oppressions. Of these latter he grows more and more painfully conscious until in his latest novel he makes them the most offensive agents of that devil who takes the hindmost. The individual worker is caught between him and the deep sea of capitalism.

Here is where Dos Passos rests his case for the present. He has found that he cannot take up arms against a sea of troubles and by opposing end them. Action cannot trammel up the consequences. And this is only one of various problems that confront him. Shall he give full vent to his sensitiveness as an artist or shall he be the pseudo-scientist and play with the thesis of determinism? Can he, in fact, choose to be the artist or do mysterious forces impel him to be the literal recorder? Must he continue to see life in all its sordidness or can he contrive an escape from it all? The doubts raised by such questions led me to refer to him at the outset as an unresolved dilemma. Certain impatient critics have protested that he is disillusioned because he no longer accepts the social program to which they are committed. He has always been disillusioned in his feeling that there is more gloom than glamour in the contemporary scene. He has written significant historical documents; he is himself a significant historical type. Until, however, through poetic or philosophical insight he comes to some clearer convictions he cannot rise above his present state of reporter rather than interpreter or prophet.

XII
Thomas Wolfe

IN HIS twenty-eighth year, after a youth in Asheville, North Carolina, college experience in the state university, a year at Harvard, and extended residence in Paris and London, Thomas Wolfe completed an autobiographical manuscript of about 350,000 words. After one rejection it fell into the hands of a hospitable editor, and in six months author and editor had fitted, changed, and compromised it into a book. This was *Look Homeward, Angel*.

It was the story of Thomas Wolfe, under the name of Eugene Gant, in his successive phases on the way to young manhood. They mark "the blind steps and gropings of his exile, the painting of his hunger, as, remembering speechlessly, he sought the great forgotten language, the lost lane-end into heaven." As he expressed his immense gusto for living, "his turbulent and undisciplined rhetoric acquired, by the regular convention of its usage, something of the movement and directness of classical epithet: his similes were preposterous, created really in the spirit of vulgar mirth and the great comic intelligence that was in the family"; for there was in him a "mad, original, disturbing quality." At sixteen "he was a child who had looked much on pain and evil and remained a fantasist of the Ideal. . . . . He was not a child when he reflected, but when he dreamt, he was; and it was the child and dreamer that governed his belief. He belonged, perhaps, to an older and simpler race of men; he belonged to the Mythmakers." Believing this of himself "he believed that the supreme ecstasy which mastered him . . . . might some day fuse its enormous light into a single articulation." At twenty he had asserted, but not achieved, his emancipation from his family, had come to the point of asking himself if perhaps he was no genius, and then of dismissing the doubt as blasphemy. "I am, he thought, a part of all I have touched and that has touched me, which having for me no existence save that which I gave to it, became other than itself by being mixed with what I then was, and is now still otherwise, having fused with what I am now, which is itself a cumulation of what I have been becoming."

Construed in this fashion, the reader may find a central purpose and a guiding principle in *Look Homeward, Angel* very much as he finds, or imagines he finds, a harmony in his own life and in the eternal scheme of things. In the philosophy of the idealist one hitches his wagon to a star, seeing relations between the homeliest acts and the sublimest laws. In the works of Wolfe the divergent elements are related to a control, though a control which ranges from the controlling forces of the stellar system to the fist of the peddler which clutches the strings of a cluster of toy balloons.

In the course of the next five years, startled by the general tenor of favorable criticism and shocked by the violence of the home-town folk, who felt that he had traduced them, he settled down to produce a second book. This had the history of a spiral nebula, starting in chaos, accumulating a vast array of unassimilated matter, and finally taking something like coherent form. Then the patient and gifted editor stepped in again, insisted that a million and a half words be assembled into sequence, insisted on cutting them and another half-million that were written as necessary links, reduced the product to about one-fifth of the total, persuaded Wolfe to stop tinkering and patching, sent the manuscript to press when his back was turned, and saw it through to publication. This was *Of Time and the River*, of the making of which, according to Mr. Maxwell Perkins, "some of it was fantastic, some was incredible, and all astonishing."

Of Time and the River is an explicitly autobiographical novel like its forerunner. In this second instalment Eugene Gant discovers himself as he leaves home, moves into a succession of new surroundings, measures them by his native standards, and finds them wanting. He has lived lustily, primitively, furiously, and he cannot endure people who have curbed their primitive lusts and furies. He goes to Harvard and encounters there a young elegant, Francis Starwick, who has the gift of endowing any word, gesture, or act with a kind of distinction. He is charmed and repelled, torn between liking and resentment. His uncouth uncle, Bascom Pentland, though fantastic and raucous, appeals to him more than his new acquaintance. He works for a while in the celebrated playwriting course at the college, and, though fascinated by his urbane and worldly instructor, feels nothing but contempt for the preciosity of his fellow-students, "false, trivial, glib, empty without substance, lacking faith." He encounters a less prosperous family who in their way, he sees, are false, foolish, and hypocritical, yet, finding nothing in them to envy, he credits them with a "courage and integrity that would not die."

He goes for a week-end visit to a great estate up the Hudson and at first glance finds there an incredible fulfilment of a dream of wealth and its proper uses. He is stirred to his depths by the beauty of the estate, the sumptuousness of the mansion. His young host is a radiant friend of humankind, the sister "unbelievably good and beautiful," the grandfather a distinguished gentleman of the old school. The guests and friends have their human limitations, but not offensively. And then suddenly, because he becomes aware that these people live within a frame of social convention—including deference to old age—he is outraged at the whole system, condemns it now as monstrous and now as unreal, admits that he is an alien from it all, and decides that he must look for "the grand life" among the brutal swarms of the city streets. He has already proved that he is a stranger to the privileged classes by his gaping wonder at the size of the estate, the splendor of the home, and the detailed equipments of bathroom, kitchen, and refrigerator; he has demonstrated that he does not understand the speech or manners of such folk by describing two of the women as quarreling like fishwives in the presence of family and guests and attributing to them the harsh idioms and voices of the Gants and the Pentlands. Yet he rejects them because of the heartlessness of their wealth and the hollowness of their etiquette and returns, defiantly unhappy, to the squalor of the city, where the grand life may exist but where he never reveals it.

He goes to Oxford, resents the fact that the dons do not mistake him for a student, and, among all the Americans he meets there, responds only to a New York Jew who sums up his sentiments about Oxford and the English with, "To hell wit' it! I'll be glad when it's all over! I'm sorry that I ever came!" True to form, when he now lodges with the Coulson's, whom he characterizes as "exiled, lost and ruined people," he likes them all. When he goes to the Continent he disparages the French, though he enjoys their restaurants. Here he meets Francis Starwick again, and again is charmed and repelled by him as he is even more acutely by a Boston woman whom he loves, loathes, vilifies, and dismisses with violent gutter talk. After a series of anticlimactic experiences he returns to America, for which distance has ever made his heart grow fonder.

The Web and the Rock, Thomas Wolfe's third. novel and the first to be posthumously published, follows the pattern of the previous two, which themselves form one whole. He had the same tale to tell, and he retells it with the names changed. The boy comes from the hill country to a southern college, goes to New York, goes to Europe, returns to teach in a metropolitan college, and all the while struggles toward self-realization as a writer. The Boston-Cambridge chapter of his life is omitted, but one long dictographic conversation is almost literally repeated and one jape originally ascribed to the playwrighting students at Harvard is now re-uttered in the foyer of an East Side "arty" theater. The author declares in his Foreword, "This novel, then, marks not only a turning away from the books I have written in the past, but a genuine spiritual and artistic change. It is the most objective novel I have written." Though this may be, the resemblance to the others shows that the difference is one of degree and not of kind. The real distinction is suggested in the opening sentence of the Foreword. "This novel is about one man's discovery of life and of the world." George Webber, its central character, has more of an eye for the world than Eugene Gant ever has. Eugene develops some fine and some funny resentments at it, but no real zest for it. George sees the juvenility of his fierce resolve not to "truckle" to more favored people and sets about to find his congenial niche. To do this he has to compound the conflict between his rural affections and his urban leanings. He has to abandon the country for the town, and yet in the town he has to compose his rural nature with his urban life. He must be a southerner in New York, and a successful southerner. Moreover, if he is to maintain his southernness he must know it in distinction to the natures of people from other regions. Hence, he must understand his America.

It is not easy to harmonize Wolfe's comments on his country and countrymen because, like all lyric passages, each is written intensely in its own mood and from the viewpoint of the moment. Old Catawba itself (North Carolina) has real character because it is redeemed and modified by northern and western qualities in contrast with South Carolina and particularly Charleston. It does not rely on the distinction of a past which, after all, was not so very distinguished. It makes no boast of age or ancestry, but in a homely way it broods over the great issues and is willing to fight for a principle. On the other hand, it has neither the certainty nor the tradition of New England and hence has never achieved the calm beauty of the New England town. Yet it is more secure than the West, a region of far distances, splendid ranges, and wanderings into the realms of the undiscovered.

These are the values ascribed to common men in rural surroundings; but to the rural boy there is something else to reckon with in America—the great legendary city, the maelstrom that has engulfed so many an ambitious youth and so many an ostentatious fortune-spender. In prospect this is a fairyland of lights and food and noise and display and comfort and fabulous people. In reality it is, on the one side, a "kind of concentration of our total energies, of the blind velocity of the period, cruel, ruthless, savage, swift, bewildering as America"; and, on the other, a sordid collection of thwarted people swarming together in darkness and dirt and loneliness and despair. To the stranger it can offer a haven of refuge from Somewhere Else, but in its immensity it offers oblivion, too. But, finally, to the true child of the city it can be a "universe of life . . . . the most human place on earth because it has in it the most 'humanity,' the most American because it has in it the most Americans." All the grandeur and base desire, the terror and innocence, the huge accomplishment and incompleteness of it, make it all-American. For him who can perceive it, the city may have the abiding strength of the plains and mountains.

Here, then, are two matters of interest in connection with Thomas Wolfe: One is himself and the degree of his adjustment to his fellows and his surroundings. The other is the method of expressing his ideas about life and his relationship to it.

It seems never to have occurred to him that he was one of a generation and that he was seeing what his generation saw; or that there was any valid point of view from which to see life except that of one who shared his particular experiences, likings, and prejudices and who found release only in the "fury" to which he was continually recurring. As a matter of fact, he confused a deep distrust and dissatisfaction with himself with a corresponding dissatisfaction with life. If he had thought less furiously and more clearly, he might have avoided confusing himself with all life and have identified himself with his "lost generation," who represent not all youth but the youth of his historic period. But, thinking of himself as a universal character, he felt that his reaction to life could be honestly and effectively expressed only in violent protest. This is in fact a perennial attitude of youth. The lyrics of the poets could fill a stout anthology of laments that the world was out of joint and with resolves either to set it right or to retire from it to some rose-embowered cottage in the vale. Wolfe was not only a youth but a raw back-country youth, and an untutored one. He read enormously, it is true, but so enormously that he could have grasped little of what passed before his eyes. His "deliberate understatement" of having read twenty thousand books in ten years laid claim to an average of almost six a day; and at the rate at which he caroused and talked and wrote during those days it allowed perhaps an average of ninety minutes to a book. That is not reading; it is rioting; and it was bound to leave him sweaty and disheveled and undisciplined in mind and mood. Resentful at the young people who had enjoyed "advantages" for which he felt more envy than contempt, and furious in his desire to suck the marrow out of whole libraries, he quite naturally felt lonely, lost, frustrated, ostracized, exiled.

In failing to identify himself with his generation, Wolfe failed to recognize the nature of the times in which he and they were living. The loneliness of the post-adolescent is grave enough while it lasts; but it is trebly intensified by the insecurities of an age which is adrift without nautical instruments or any system of dead reckoning by which to seek a harbor. All his wild pawing of books had been too casual to reveal to him that each great book had been the precipitate of an age in which certain common convictions prevailed or that, while these convictions shifted from age to age, there had always prevailed some dominant set in terms of which literature was understandable. He did not realize that though every period is a period of transition, his period was to an extraordinary degree a period of unbelief and nonbelief, lying between a time of actual loss and a time of potential recovery. And so he wrote, "We walk the streets of life alone." "Why here? Why there? Why now? Why then?" "O lost, and by the wind grieved." "Let me look upon the living face of darkness." "A young man is so strong, so mad, so certain, and so lost."

If it be considered an error to attribute to Wolfe the characteristics he ascribed to Eugene Gant and George Webber, he has supplied the grounds for it in various passages. The Preface to *Look Homeward, Angel* contended that any serious novel must be autobiographical, using and fusing material derived from the author's experience. *The Story of a Novel* reasserted this and went on to give as literal autobiography the basic experiences told about Eugene and to be told of George. The "Author's Note" to *The Web and the Rock*, which is about the "whole adventure of apprenticeship and discovery" says the tale contains a "strong element of satiric exaggeration" because this is an element of American life. Once again he identifies himself with his work; for the satiric exaggeration is not a trait of his characters but a feature of his method in presenting them.

He was young Byron, which means that he had with Byron's self-pity his abundance of vitality, his poetic gift, and, withal, his vulgarity. This was expressed by both in wanton challenge to the conventional people whom they chose to ruffle; but Byron's was the vulgarity of a member of the House of Lords and Wolfe's the vulgarity of a North Carolina hill-villager. Byron never descended to Billingsgate; Wolfe was brought up on it. Byron was suavely depraved at times; Wolfe was often foully obscene. There may be little to choose between the moral effects of the two vulgarities, but it may be safely said that only those who are used to foul obscenity can relish it at length. Herein, again, is the difference between the resort to the vulgar in Wolfe and Steinbeck. Wolfe did give the impression of relishing it, ascribing it repeatedly and at length to his central characters. Steinbeck occasionally puts a four-letter noun or epithet into the speech of his characters, but only to characterize them and usually with the implication that they are quite unconscious of what they are saying. The effects are totally different; and the lengths to which Wolfe went can be no better indicated than by the fact that even his sympathetic but sensitive editor now and then took refuge in those emphasizing skeletoned words at which Emerson demurred a hundred years ago when he protested to his journal, "I hate a sham damn."

To turn from the man to his method, few writers of marked defects have attained such distinction. The title, *Of Time and the River*, is used to describe not the novel, for which a title is normally chosen, but the artist and his demon. Time as applied to the problem is threefold: the actual present, which the artist uses in his fable; the recent past, of which the actors and events are the final issue; and all eternity, past and future, against which the transitory beings in the fable are projected. The river is a double concept: a vast tide of things, people, and events surging through the artist's memory, and an irresistible force impelling him to mold them into a design. And the river in this second sense is a demon, a driving spirit forcing him not to think or to dream but to cover paper with words in undirected bursts of energy; a demon, which in another metaphor is a storm cloud "pouring from its depths a torrential and ungovernable flood." All the while, as the words piled up season after season, Wolfe, furiously at work, was harried by day and hag-ridden by night with "dreams of Guilt and Time" because he felt abysmally guilty of wasting his time, unfaithful to his trust, unable to persuade himself, like his admired fellow-writer James Joyce, that he was performing "work in progress."

His central theme was to find the "image of a strength and wisdom external to his need and superior to his hunger, to which the belief and power of his own life could be united." If he could establish this in life he could arrive at a unifying principle in his work. But at this point he was baffled by conflicting ideas as to how life could be transmitted into fiction. On the one hand, he conceived of life under the general heading of "Amount and Number." He could make endless lists of places, persons, things, and events he had glimpsed, and thus glimpsing had built into himself because he was a part of all he had encountered. He could subdivide and re-enumerate each of these lists so that places became continents, countries, states, cities, towns, landscapes and seascapes, churches, shops, stores, street-corners, dwellings, rooms, and all the details of each elaborated in "minutely thorough, desperately evocative descriptions." But, on the other hand, these minute descriptions, microcosmic in detail, became impossibly immense in bulk. After long struggles he arrived for himself at the fundamental discovery that the novelist might imply as well as describe, that the demon had goaded him into "intemperate excess," and that a few characters, rightly depicted, might best convey a sense of the million-footed city.

Unreconciled to a world which seems all the more chaotic because of his frequent exultant bursts of momentary delight, he naturally was influenced by men of like temper, not only in point of view, but more especially in form. He acknowledged James Joyce, though the debt was slight, for Joyce had no critical attitude toward the world and took refuge in what Wolfe lacked—a highly elaborated technique. He found a model, or a vindication, in Dostoevski, for the turbulent confusion in which he struggled and which he communicated to the reader. "*Crime and Punishment*," he wrote, "seemed to boil outward from some secret, unfathomable, and subterranean source; . . . . seemed to weave out upon a dark and turbulent tide of feeling. . . . . It was all too hard and confusing to follow."

Wolfe was also an enthusiast for Walt Whitman.

"This was my meadow," he wrote of Whitman's metropolis. "I walked about in it. These faces were my blades of grass." Hence the resemblance in both centripetal philosophy and fragmentary scheme of composition. Wolfe resorted, like Whitman, to the inventory device, listing sights on a journey, odors from every source and season, the contents of libraries, his readings—the great lyrics and dramas, the epic masterpieces, the more recondite works, the adventure tales, the sources of metaphor, and the heroic characters of the past who, taken together, were the fulfilments of his own imagined but potential self. These are mere catalogues of related details; sometimes there were groups forming a series of series, completer units like the successive strophes of Whitman's invertebrate longer poems: grouped parodies of romantic fiction with himself each time in the central role, laboriously elaborated picture sequences of events that were transpiring in an afternoon hour, an after-midnight hour, an early morning hour, either in actual America or in the luxurious daydreamings of the adolescent mind.

Allied to these are undirected stream-of-consciousness passages, starting from some word or event in the tale and running on in spotty, exclamatory fragments. They occur now and then, not consistently enough or frequently enough to stand out as a feature of Wolfe's style. More characteristic are the recurrent lyric passages which appear so often in his pages that a fraction of them have been excerpted and published in the volume called *The Face of a Nation*. These are pure poetry, Whitman-like, yet indubitably not Whitman but Wolfe. All have the fundamental quality of poetry that they are specific in phrasing but general in significance, and more significant in what they imply than in what they declare.

Finally, though there is no clear debt, there is a marked resemblance between Wolfe and Mark Twain. It appears in the satiric exaggeration which Wolfe acknowledges in *The Web and the Rock*, with the explanation that it belongs particularly to the nature of American life. This belongs most particularly to the rural westerner come to town. It belongs to a period which was Mark Twain's but which lingered in the hinterland long after it had passed in the older East. It is the tone of Mark Twain in *Innocents Abroad*, and it is adopted by Thomas Wolfe when he sees either the East or Europe. It is the tone of the rude raconteur who somewhat labors his points, encouraged by the rude laughter of his auditors. And it enjoys the perpetration of the literary hoax and the oral practical joke. Eugene Gant visits an obscure widow and daughter in a Boston suburb and entertains himself over an entire season with monstrous tales about his family.

Thomas Wolfe

He wanders about Paris and records the silly talk of
the American traveler. The town boys gang up on
George Webber in a scene which is like an episode
rejected from the *Tom Sawyer* manuscript. A burlesque on a school graduation by Wolfe reads like an
unpublished passage from Mark Twain. Wolfe may
not have imitated Mark Twain, but he often reverted to the nineteenth-century horseplay in which
Sam Clemens was schooled.

Thomas Wolfe was not playing mock modest
when he confessed to the intemperate excess of
which critics had accused him and to the waste,
error, and confusion to which this led him. He was
of all things honest about himself, and we may accept both his honesty and his critical fairness when
he declared, "I am not a professional writer; I am
not even a skilled writer; I am just a writer who is
on the way to learning his profession. . . . . I don't
know how to write a story yet. I don't know how
to write a novel yet. But I have learned something
about myself and about the work of writing." Yet
it is deeply significant that he should constantly
offer reminders of such titans as Whitman and Mark
Twain. They were both of the people, both deeply
resentful of what confronted them in daily life. To
Whitman, life in America was a "mad chaos." To
Mark Twain, the world was peopled by the

"damned human race." Both had given over the old orthodoxy, were trying to find the meaning of things, Mark Twain ending in total despair, Whitman in total optimism. Wolfe, who resembled them at so many points, was nearer to Whitman than to Mark Twain in his conclusions; and his writing up to the time of his death was as casually structureless as theirs. One of them was anecdotal and fragmentary, the other, lyric and fragmentary. Wolfe was anecdotal and lyric and fragmentary.

At the same time he had their fierce energy, their tender love of beauty, and their outreaching sense of time and space:

"Thus did he see first, he the hill-bound, the sky-girt, of whom the mountains were his masters, the fabulous South. The pictures of flashing field, of wood, and hill, stayed in his heart forever. . . . .

"The commonness of all things in the earth he remembered with a strange familiarity—he dreamed of the quiet roads, the moonlit woodlands, and he thought that some day he would come to them on foot, and find them there unchanged, in all the wonder of recognition. They had existed for him anciently and forever.

"Eugene was almost twelve years old."

"And day came, and the song of waking birds, and the Square, bathed in the young pearl light of morning. And a wind stirred lightly in the Square, and, as he looked, Ben, like a fume of smoke, was melted in the Square.

"And the Angels on Gant's porch were frozen in hard marble silence, and at a distance life awoke, and there was a rattle of lean wheels, a slow clangor of shod hoofs. And he heard the whistle wail along the river.

"Yet, as he stood for the last time by the angels of his father's porch, it seemed as if the Square were already far and lost; or, I should say, he was like a man who stands upon a hill above the town he has left, yet does not say 'The town is near,' but turns his eyes upon the distant soaring ranges."

I have quoted Wolfe's strictures on himself and accepted them as just. I accept also his statement, "He belonged, perhaps to an older and simpler race of men; he belonged to the Mythmakers."

You Can't Go Home Again, Wolfe's second and final posthumous novel, serves as a capstone for his work. Once again he made himself the central character, using once more his second alias, George Webber, and concluding this conclusion with a forty-page epitome of his total experience. Only the reader who is familiar with his other novels and with *The Story of a Novel* can appreciate the completeness of this self-analysis. In Wolfe's opinion he was a changed and matured writer. Time still drove him relentlessly, but Amount and Number, though they might harass him, did not overwhelm him. He was, he believed, so transformed by maturity that he could not go back to his childhood or to the home of his youth or to his youthful dreams or to his old detachment from the hideous events that were transforming his world. He must become an evangelist and strive not to restore America to its lost estate but to find a new future for it. He must use all his experiences for more than themselves to establish a truth more true than any fact he had ever encountered. In the most splendid of lyric passages he abjured lyricism and dedicated his powers to democracy. *You Can't Go Home Again* records this resolution, but it reveals no new powers. It is the concluding chapter of a story begun long ago. It is idle to speculate on what might have happened in the sequel; for soon after its completion Thomas Wolfe died.

XIII

Ole Edvart Rölvaag

T HE more an author," writes Glenway Wes-
cott, "has in common with his characters,
the better; typical trivialities surpass in significance the noblest feelings; an immediate report
is more valuable than reminiscences, the rest is lyricism. . . . . No judicious novelist will strive to out-
distance life; he will choose problems which only
seem insoluble, which in some corner of society, in
some small illustrative scale, have been solved. The
future of America is a genuine riddle. The riddle of
a sphinx with the perfect face of a movie star."
The passage is pertinent to the Norwegian-American Rölvaag, who had everything in common with
his characters and whose trilogy proceeded to the
third generation, grandchildren of immigrant stock
merged in a civilization which popularly idealized
the face of the sphinx, whether it was Buster Kea-
ton's, Bill Hart's, or Calvin Coolidge's.

The Norwegian immigration seems to have been
the last considerable one to sweep over the West. It
was not until after the Civil War that the Scandina-
vians made their way into South Dakota, where

their offspring now amount to a third of the population. At the last reported census more than a million born in Norway or of Norwegian parentage lived in the six north-central states. As three-fourths of these have belonged to rural life, they have been peculiarly free to foster the language and traditions of the homeland. Harsh circumstance forced them to take bodily leave of the old country. Grateful and hopeful in the new world, their hearts were still in Norway. As they are a literate people, they became prolific in authorship, publishing in their own tongue for their own people on both sides of the Atlantic. Two of the names most often associated with their migration do not really belong to it: Johann Bojer, because he has been a European observer, and H. H. Boyesen, because in his American career he did not cast in his lot with the immigrants but joined the eastern professoriate and wrote his stories in English.

But there have been scores upon scores of journalists and hundreds of contributors to poets' corners—little corners of sentimental Norway tucked off in corners of the Northwest, and a smaller and more significant number of travel writers and novelists. Prevailing in their pages is the consciousness of the pilgrim and the sojourner. Often the title-page reveals that the literary waif was privately printed: in Iowa City, in Ephraim, Wisconsin, in Watford

City, North Dakota. Other works were issued from Norwegian presses: the Amundsen Company, Decorah, Iowa, the Augsburg Publishing House, Minneapolis, the International Press or the Heiborg Printing House in New York and Brooklyn; or with Aschehoug and Company, Oslo. Almost without exception the two lands are linked together in the stories: A poor boy comes to America, thrives, and returns to claim his sweetheart and wreak vengeance on a Norwegian oppressor; a poor boy comes to America, sends for his sweetheart, and reaches the high goal of the pulpit; a poor boy comes to America and has a daughter who rebels at the sordidness of Jonasville, another Gopher Prairie, and, going to Chicago, marries one Miles Standish Ward; a poor boy comes to America and makes his fortune but declines into spiritual bankruptcy; another Norwegian, a sculptor, strives to find his place in the American scene; and one, like Rölvaag himself, develops into a solid, courageous citizen, bent on contributing the best of Norwegian character to the nation of his adoption.

To this tide of fiction from O. A. Buslett, Peer Stromme, Waldemar Ager, Simon Johnson, and H. A. Foss, Ole Edvart Rölvaag contributed his *Letters from America, The Forgotten Path, Two Fools, The Ship of Longing.* But to name them thus is misleading, for like all the others by this group they were published in Norwegian for Norwegians, though in the United States. Then came throughout the reading world a new vogue for the novel of the soil, accelerated by Hamsun's influence; then also in the United States a fresh zest for frontier tales; and then, finally, the announcement that Bojer was planning to treat the theme of the Norwegian immigrant on the American plains. This was an unconscious challenge to Rölvaag which he promptly accepted. In 1924, within a month of each other, the two novels were published in Norwegian. Not till three years later was *Giants in the Earth* issued in an English version. Within a twelvemonth this ran to forty-four printings. It was the first of a trilogy of which *Peder Victorious* and *Their Fathers' God* were the later members, and the apparent interruption of the sequence with *Pure Gold* is misleading, for this was a translation of *To Tullinger* (Two Fools), a story of a decade earlier.

Rölvaag's equipment for writing this chronicle of transition from Norway to America traced through three generations was complete. He had reached manhood when he came over from the old country. He put himself through school and college in short order, sharing in the life of his fellow-immigrants. In early maturity he was launched on teaching Norwegian language and literature in St. Olaf's College, which was founded for the education of the children of Norway, and he was an active and influential man in the church. From now on his interests were twofold: to keep alive the faith of his fathers and to conserve the cultural heritage from the old land which the younger generation in their readiness to become Americanized were tempted to treat as a mess of pottage.

An exceptional man, Rölvaag afforded exceptions, without overthrowing them, to two broad and valid generalizations about frontier life and frontier literature. According to F. J. Turner's "law" the wilderness masters the colonist and transforms him into a new American product. It did so with Rölvaag but left him an exception to the rule by mastering him without overwhelming him. Again, it is the usual case in frontier evolution that when the pioneer becomes articulate he writes literature for the frontier but not about it, or if he writes about it he converts it into a circus or a masquerade or a sentimental drama.

Rölvaag compressed wide breadth and variety into a single career. Not content with a complete mastery of two languages and a blending of two cultures, he progressed from the life of the toiler to the life of the scholar and thence to the life of the artist. Even at that, as artist he composed in his native tongue, relying for his English versions on free translation under close supervision. He was what Natty Bumppo Cooper might have been, or better still, Antonia Shimerda Cather, if such characters could have lived and written. He not only saw all that he wrote about; it was all in the warp of his emotional experience and found its natural expression in the language he heard as a child. When he wrote, therefore, he was not the frontiersman trying to handle a pen with his trigger finger or a Joaquin Miller in sombrero and boots at a London salon. He was the only kind of novelist who could vie with Johann Bojer and surpass him, for he was the primitive subject of Bojer's *The Emigrants*, and he was also Bojer's peer as a creative writer.

The fundamental approaches of the two novelists are apparent at a reading. Bojer wrote as a European about emigrants; Rölvaag as an American about immigrants. Rölvaag had lived what Bojer had heard about even more remotely than Miss Cather did. Bojer made a leisurely start with Morten Kvidal in Dyrendal and returned there with him in the concluding pages. He was a Norwegian author, aware of the lure of the Northwest for legions of his countrymen, interested enough in it to have posted himself on the essential and more or less superficial facts. But to the end his attitude toward his material was that of the home-stayer who listens with fascinated attention to the tales of a traveler. It is all very extraordinary, he seems to say, the voyage, the last slow journey over the prairie, the locating of the claim, the ground-breaking, the raising of the first crops, the numbing experiences of heat and cold, pest and fire, and withal the steady progress toward freedom and fortune. He is so absorbed in a thousand unfamiliar events and circumstances that he feels

> no need of a remoter charm
> By thought supplied, nor any interest
> Unborrowed from the eye.

Only in the closing paragraphs does he convey the idea that there are epic implications in all this.

In contrast, Rölvaag's participation in the action gives his treatment of the theme an emotional depth that could not be native to Bojer. The narrative undertaking to which the writer-immigrant set himself was the kind already approached by Buslett, Ager, and the others: to present through an immediate report the double ordeal of the alien of another country and a foreign speech. He must not only break the kinship of the soul, and the soil on which it has grown (the pioneer from the eastern states or the British Isles has done that); he must also cope with a new language. Yet genuinely to acquire a new speech demands, as Rölvaag once wrote in a rare moment of epistolary self-interpretation, ''a spiritual adjustment which is forever beyond the power of the average man because it requires a re-making of soul. He cannot give up the old, because that would mean death to him, and he cannot master the new—the process is simply beyond his powers. This is a phase of national assimilation that any American, or any Norwegian, can grasp intellectually; but only the Norwegian-American who has survived the struggle can grasp and present its emotional verity. The physical conquest of a wilderness leaves the immigrant no time or energy for language study, and acquiring a language means far more than building up a workaday vocabulary. The complete transition from one country to another can come only with so intimate a mastery of the new speech that the emotional life may find spontaneous outlet through the new medium. And that is the miracle of acquiring a new soul which only one in ten thousand can achieve.''

It is the tragedy inherent in this situation that leads to the conquest over the pioneer—to Turner's brief statement that the wilderness masters the colonist. The immigrant pioneer is confronted by peril on peril: first, of physical defeat while he and his kind are transforming the surface of the earth; then, as the community closes around him, of social submergence without inner adjustment; finally, if he have the capacity for gaining a new soul which is forever beyond the powers of the average, of the

Ole Edvart Rölvaag

ostracism that penalizes independence or the surrender to Mammon that follows material success in the midst of small-town Philistinism. One can trace the succession of these catastrophes on the chief figures in the Rölvaag chronicle.

Regarding *Giants in the Earth* and *Peder Victorious* as parts of a single narrative, the natural division falls not between the covers of the two books, but in the middle of the first volume with the end of the section called "The Land Taking." This is a tale of primitive life which can be considered wholly in folk terms. Per Hansa, the hero, is the incarnation of primitive strength. He builds largest, plows longest, sows earliest, laughs loudest, rages most wildly, forgives most generously. He is pre-eminent in all performance. His wife, Beret, is primitive fear. She is in perpetual terror of punishment for surrender before wedlock, harassed by the thought of unfaith to the land she has abandoned, saddled with all the burdens of both Christian and pagan superstitition. Most of all the prairie overwhelms her by its vast reach and ominous silence. In this folk story the prairie itself is primitive nature, the earth-spirit so familiar to a people who have always had to contend with it—no South-European Ceres. "From eternity the prairie had lain here, lapping sun and drinking moisture, and had peered up into

an endless blue day, brimful to running over. At
evening it had listened to strange tales told by the
twilight breeze. But now other concerns had come
to occupy the thoughts of the Great Plain, giving it
not so much as a moment of rest. The sod huts
crumbled and merged again with the earth out of
which they had come. Sod is but sod, after all, and
was never meant to shelter human beings so long as
they can stand on their legs. . . . . Large dwellings
and huge barns sprang up all over. Summers the
Great Plain tried tornadoes; in spring and autumn,
prairie fires, until heaven and earth roared in one
blaze; during the winter she would let loose all the
deviltry she could think of, by way of raging bliz-
zards, spewing out a horror of snow and cold. But
all in vain; the houses reared themselves faster than
she could destroy them. Even the elements had to
learn that the power of man had to be respected,
especially when energized by a great joy."

For a while Per Hansa, apparent conqueror of the
plains, lacks strength to contend with the ominous
and incessant forebodings of Beret. It takes more
than muscle to withstand fears that only intellect
and emotion can dispel. The great joy that comes
with the birth of Peder restores both man and wife.
Immediate and overwhelming disaster is averted,
and the newcomer brings an assurance that the monster of the plains cannot always prevail. But Beret's

blended orthodoxy and superstition drive Per Hansa
out into a blizzard in search for a cleric to perform
extreme unction for a dying relative. He goes for
God's emissary in vain defiance of demonic nature
and never returns. At last Beret regains her balance
with the aid of the final myth element to enter the
tale, the primitive faith embodied in the parson,
spokesman for the Most High, in whose voice is
heard the reassurance of the intercessor. She is reserved for a less elemental role in the ensuing story
and for a less elemental, though no less positive,
defeat.

Analysis expresses itself in abstract terms; creative art, with the concrete. Critical analysis is
bound, therefore, to do violence to the object of its
attention. Yet the harsh process must be followed a
step further in a word of summary. *Giants in the
Earth* is a twofold story. I have suggested the essen-
tials of the first part in terms of primitive ethnology:
man and nature in their eternal conflict; man, as part
of the tide of human life inexorably sure of success;
man, the individual, ephemeral as the grass of the
field. In "The Land Taking" the conflict is presented, the sentence is pronounced alike on human
strength and human weakness, but Peder Victorious
is born. Man falls in the taking of the land, but his
seed survives for "The Founding of the Kingdom."

The second part now becomes a more complex and

sophisticated tale of community life, not to be interpreted in the same terms—no longer recounting a conflict against nature or natural fears, predestined to ultimate success but pursuing the later problem of whether man who can subdue the monster of the plains can also adjust his own nature to the stream of circumstance. It is a connecting link with the succeeding volume, the story of Peder himself.

The Grand Canyon yawns no deeper than the chasm between successive generations with its opposing walls of convention and revolt. Between parents and children of immigrant stock it is wider than normal, even when the newcomers share the language of the new country. But when there is the added cleavage of speech, the abyss may become too broad for any but the most tenuous of bridges. *Peder Victorious* presents this tragic alienation between mother and child. They lose all sense of intimacy: he cannot understand her songs; he cannot take the nourishment on which her soul has thrived. And more poignant than his loss is hers, for she sees him slip away into an alien fastness where she may not follow because she has not the key and cannot learn the password. The concluding scene in *Giants in the Earth* is of Per Hansa in the horrible dissolution of death, struck down by the monster of the plain. The concluding scene in *Peder Victorious* is of Mother Beret bending to the inevitable.

(236)

Ole Edvart Rölvaag

Her son, promise of the future, is advancing to meet it, speaking the strange tongue of a new land, marrying the strange offspring of another land, their son to be American born of American born. For Beret there is no alternative but acceptance of his choice or resistance that will lead to total estrangement, and the decision is inevitable. Once more, and in another way, the pioneer is overcome even while in the act of creating a new America.

It remained, then, for Rölvaag to deal with the children of the pioneers, who were sloughing off the ways and the traditions of Europe. Their own were in the making; and they were making them in Gopher Prairie, in Winesburg, in Zenith, in Spoon River, just as farther east they were remaking them in Robert Frost's region north of Boston or in Robinson's Tilbury. There were two possibilities for Peder. The chief peril he faced was the disapproval of his neighbors with their lust for tuppenny-ha'penny prosperity and petty comfort. In their eyes the seventh and succeeding deadly sins were to disturb the market or the sanctity of the Republican party, to violate a vague and unknown Constitution, to depart from a literal interpretation of the first six chapters of the book of Genesis, or to grant others the slightest indulgence in any of these blasphemies. Peder might stand for the magnanimities, see life in the large, save his soul, but become an outcast; or he might adjust himself to barn and silo, windmill and tractor, and make his little fortune at the price of his soul.

Rölvaag chose the former course in a story centering about Peder's domestic life but radiating to the circumference of Norwegian-America. The thesis is developed at length by "Reverend" Kaldahl at a Christmastide party where he is a none too welcome guest. The occasion stirs him to an eloquent monologue in his native tongue which bores most of the Norwegians and is unintelligible to Peder's Irish wife, her father and brother, but is challenging enough to overcome Peder's first resistance. The parson maintains that any vital national life is rooted in tradition, that the American tradition of liberty under the law and religious freedom is largely English, and that the England of the Puritans owed its character to Scandinavian influence. He holds, therefore, that the Norwegians' best gift to the land of their adoption was not to forswear their past but to contribute the best of their tradition to American life. It is significant of the episode that he exhorts most of his countrymen in vain and makes himself foggily offensive to the immigrants from Ireland.

Transposed from speech to action, this is the upshot of Peder's experience. A child of Lutheran folk, he has derived little from the sect but the inclination to nonconformity. Under his own roof he finds that his Protestant mother and Catholic wife are fierce and primitive contenders for the soul's salvation of his baby boy, each instinctively, and unscrupulously, acting to conserve a sacred tradition. They are unreconciled when the mother dies and the wife abandons him. In public life Peder's desire to act with the independence of a true pioneer is frustrated by the indifference of the Norwegians and the hostility of the Irish. The slow, clumsy process of democratic assimilation continues, and Peder remains one of the always meager handful of his native race who are not afraid to risk their fortunes in a bold adventure. So the hard fate of Peder in an evolving world of security and comfort-seeking is as cruel as the tragedies of Per Hansa and Beret. It is the inevitable consequence of drafting the energies of a whole generation for the promotion of material ends.

One thinks back to that eighteenth-century essay in Crèvecœur's *Letters from an American Farmer* which contains a still unfulfilled prophecy of a new race fused from the nations of the old world, new men acting on new principles, entertaining new opinions, forming new opinions. It is true, as the rhapsodist predicted, that the American has caused great changes in the world. The rest may become true some day short of the millennium. In the meanwhile the fusing process is still on, and the crucible proves to be anything but a bed of roses. That is why Rölvaag, honest teller of tales, who undertook neither to idealize nor to prophesy, was bound to be a somber recorder of the successive conquests over the pioneer in the Northwest.

XIV
John Steinbeck

T O SOME of us who have been aware of John
Steinbeck since he first appeared in print he
seems to have hoed a long, hard row. Ten
years is a long time in the life of a young man. Yet
fame and fortune came to him in his late thirties,
which ought to be soon enough for any man. When
they did come at full flood with *The Grapes of Wrath*,
most of the people who wrote and talked about
him, whether in praise or blame, treated him as a
newcomer, the author of a second book. As a matter of fact, *Of Mice and Men* and *The Grapes of Wrath*
are foreshadowed in a longish sequence of earlier
works. And a striking fact about these earlier
works is that they were a series of excursions in
various directions on various themes in various
moods, though with a common trait, and that his
most popular books are externally quite different
from the earlier ones and yet share the trait common to them all in attempting to get below the surface of life and to set in play the basic elements of
human character.

His first novel, *The Cup of Gold*, appeared in 1929. Steinbeck was twenty-seven years old when he made his bow with this romance which is subtitled "A life of Sir Henry Morgan, Buccaneer, with Occasional References to History." He had worked up with evident care this account of the Scotch boy who ran away, took to the seas, served his term as an indentured servant, and quickly rose to pre-eminence as the half-legalized foe of Spain in American waters, successful enough as a pirate to win his country's gratitude, inept enough as anything but a pirate to sink under the double burden of respectable marriage and royal favor. This is in the vein of light satire, and there is much of light satire in the telling of the tale. But there is more than that. Henry Morgan's father is a wise and inefficient man, a friend of Merlin, sage and recluse. They predict that he will be a great man, because up to a certain point he will want the moon and will be guided toward it by a saving unintelligence. Breaking the bounds of mediocrity he commits terrible villainies. He knows other men well enough to keep them at a distance and play upon their fears, cupidities, lusts, and vanities. He cares for them too little to be tied by any loyalty. And when he has captured Panama, "the cup of gold," and has the incomparable woman of legend in his power, he discovers that he has suddenly grown up, that the moon is a bubble, and he returns to mediocrity and the "giant duty" of appearances, having lost his overmastering desires. Merlin's sage saying has been fulfilled: "You are a little boy. You want the moon to drink from as a golden cup; and so it is very likely that you will become a great man—if only you remain a little child. . . . . But if one grow to a man's mind, that mind must see that it cannot have the moon and would not want it if it could."

It is a good tale vividly told, full of life and color, with an underlying humor which is now grave and now puckish, and it shows a mastery of prose that boys of twenty-seven seldom achieve. If the depression had not crashed on *The Cup of Gold*, it might have won many readers for its successor. But they would have been disappointed; for Steinbeck never again wrote in this exact vein, and from then on he seldom worked the same vein twice.

So *The Pastures of Heaven*, which appeared three years later, abandoned the old world and the past and the use of the library, though he had demonstrated how well he could use these resources. It was a set of tales and sketches about various types, normal and abnormal, who lived in a valley in the Far West. People began to compare Steinbeck to Thornton Wilder—that was because of the poetry and the fantasy; and to William Faulkner—that was because of the mordant quality in some of the tales. Certain critics were enthusiastic, but he gained few readers. Nor did his public grow appreciably with his next and more remarkable, *To a God Unknown*.

With *To a God Unknown* critics began to compare Steinbeck to D. H. Lawrence. That is because of his emphasis upon the god of fecundity and because, even though they called it his "most powerful and mature work," they were somewhat bewildered by the maturity of this man of thirty and suggested a literary obligation by drawing a comparison. The novel shows kinship to the short stories in *The Pastures of Heaven*. Joseph Wayne was not after the moon; he was a passionate worshiper of the earth, a son of Ceres. Coming from impoverished Vermont and a farm too small to support his clan, he left behind him his pagan father and after settling on California soil was always followed by the paternal spirit. His father in the East had been the living symbol of man's relation to the earth. Joseph inherited that authority. When his three brothers and their wives followed him and settled on their combined acreage, he felt the joy of Abraham in the increase of his tribe and of their herds. He became a godlike part of nature, a noble pagan. One of his brothers was a wastrel and paid his life for his lust. One was an orthodox religious bigot and fought what he saw as the devil in Joseph. One was a lover of all growing creatures, a man after Joseph's own heart. When a killing drought came, it appeared as God's wrath to the bigot, but to Joseph it was the temporary withholding of Nature's riches. When he brought his young bride home, Rama, his brother's wife, expounded him to her: "I tell you this man is not a man, unless he is all men. The strength, the resistance, the long and stumbling thinking of all men, and all the joy and suffering too, cancelling each other out and yet remaining in the contents. He is all these, a repository for a little piece of each man's soul, and more than that, a symbol of the earth's soul."

Withal Steinbeck made him a simple, human figure, who could thus impress an understanding woman but who could laugh and labor and beg and worship, always a son of nature and seldom other than natural in ordinary human terms. The book is a poem, an idyll, but it is also a tale. And the eternal myth elements are in it.

Pastures of Heaven and *To a God Unknown* had enough in common to suggest that Steinbeck had "found himself"—that he had developed a kind of story and a way of telling it and that he might go on reduplicating it like a farm expert who has developed a new strain of corn. He was profound in his sympathies, acute in his understanding, and, though his sense of humor was quick and keen, he was prevailingly grave in tone. But in *The Pastures of Heaven* there is a gay sketch of the two daughters of Guiermo Lopez, "the best makers of tortillas in the valley." Near to dire penury, they sell their edibles and encourage trade by accepting the embraces of patrons with lusty appetites. Driven out by the protests of the local women, they eventually go to the city to sell favors they had previously given away. In their bland amorality they are harbingers of the three *paisanos* of *Tortilla Flat* who are as oblivious of the law and the Ten Commandments as the characters in another book of the period, *February Hill*. The *paisanos* are vaguely conceivable in their laugh-provoking irresponsibility, but unreal as sprites or gnomes. *Tortilla Flat* is something between fantasy, burlesque, and farce. The author was as irresponsible as his characters. He may have been bored by critics who were beginning to read unintended meanings into his tales, for twice he took flings at painstaking interpreters:

"Pilon complained, 'It is not a good story. There are too many meanings and too many lessons in it. Some of those lessons are opposite. There is not a story to take into your head. It proves nothing.'

" 'I like it,' said Pablo. 'I like it because it hasn't any meaning you can see, but still it does seem to mean something, I can't tell what.' "

And again, "Some time a historian may write a

cold, dry, fungus-like history of the party. He may refer to the moment when Danny defied and attacked the whole party. . . . . He may conclude, 'A dying organism is often observed to be capable of extraordinary endurance and strength.' . . . . But I say, and the people of Tortilla Flat would say, 'To hell with it. That Danny was a man for you!' '' Steinbeck's popularity did not increase with this book; it began with it.

Now with an audience at his beck and ready to laugh with him, the roving author turned completely away from such fantasy, as also from mysticism and romantic adventure—so far away that one cannot reconstruct from his earlier books even an ex post facto explanation for what he wrote next. The reason is doubtless to be found in his life, for he had been many kinds of wage-earner and he had seen and felt the frictions between working man and employer. At any rate he wrote on this phase of life, calling his story *In Dubious Battle*.

Again one is tempted to compare Steinbeck with other contemporaries. It is a far cry from Wilder and Lawrence and Faulkner to Frank Norris and Jack London and Upton Sinclair; yet they are the inevitable names to cite at this point, for what had taken place was the step from art to argument. Not that art was abandoned and that the argument was as explicit as in much of London and Sinclair; but art was sacrificed or subdued for the benefit of social implications. Communists have wanted to claim Steinbeck but have spoken guardedly as of one who might be too intractable for membership. However, the result of his using art for social ends is not a happy one for those who care more for the California tales about man's relation to nature than maybe Steinbeck himself continued to, as he now turned to man in his relation to the class struggle. Fantasy disappears, the poetic aura is dispelled, and the story becomes reportorial. The author refrained, as few have done under similar temptation, from interpretative expository writing; and from the introduction of known characters and events, as both Lewis and Sinclair have introduced them. But when the book is read, the reader lays it down feeling that all the carefully elaborated character portraits, dialogues, and episodes have been caught by the dictaphone and the candid camera, that their veracity is doubtless unassailable, but that they are the products of industry rather than artistry.

After this came *Of Mice and Men*, which had the same solid warp as all its predecessors but which was different on the surface pattern, the fifth kind of story by Steinbeck. It won him a fresh esteem from the critics and a new kind of popularity with strangers. Whether intended so or not it was in fact an elaborate scenario for the inevitable play which grew out of it. A dramatization of a novel is usually made by rejecting nine-tenths of the original and heavily compressing the rest. If the job is well done the novel is recognizable in its irreducible minimum as a play. *Of Mice and Men*, the tale, is of play length. It is compact and tightly unified in the classical manner. It is in essence a tragic play. Two tramp laborers come to a ranch and a job. One is a great hulking half-wit, comparable to Tularecito and Johnny Bear, and the other is a little hustler, held by loyalty to the gigantic "innocent" whom he berates and protects. Together they dream of a day when they can have their acre or two with a garden and some stock and a dry roof and security in each other's strength. But the big hulk lives through his big hands. He wants to pet mice and puppies and kills them in his fondness. He sees a red dress, wants to touch it, is alarmed into violence, and the two pals have to run for their lives. At the ranch they find a third vagrant laborer who is eager to share their dream home and has most of the few dollars needed for the purchase price. But once more big Lennie, the innocent, "does something bad." He is lured by a wanton hussy into caressing her, is frightened by her fright, and in his mighty irritation shakes her to death and runs away. His little guardian finds him before the avengers catch up and shoots him to save him from their blood lust. Out of such simple stuff, in simplest style and sequence, Steinbeck told a masterly tale. The elemental factors are there: love, lust, loyalty, natural depravity, a feeling for nature's serenity, and a yearning for peace.

The Long Valley, next in the sequence, is Steinbeck maturing, Steinbeck recognizable, but Steinbeck with a difference. For the most part he returned to the earth with no industrial machine intervening between man and man or man and nature. "The Raid" alone carries us back to Reds and Red-baiters and jungle law parading as justice. Two sketches, "The Snake" and "Johnny Bear," of a pathological woman and a gruesome, subnormal man-beast, revert to the realm of Tularecito in *The Pastures of Heaven* and the ghastly trail opened by Ambrose Bierce. "Saint Katy the Virgin" is a hilarious burlesque in the mood of *Tortilla Flat;* but most of the collection, culminating in the longest unit, "The Red Pony," deal with simple, elemental people who fulfil themselves only in relation to other living things, parts of universal life inevitably tinged with poetry. So the garrulous old man who bored his son-in-law with interminable repetitions of pioneer experiences furnishes the concluding significant passage in the book: He had been tiresome, he realized, because he had failed to express what his adventures meant to him. He wasn't really a vain babbler, he explained, "It wasn't Indians that were important, nor adventures, nor even getting out here. . . . . We carried life out here and set it down the way those ants carry eggs. And I was the leader. The westering was as big as God, and the slow steps that made the movement piled up and piled up until the continent was crossed.''

By these steps the stage was set for *Grapes of Wrath*. The story is told in fifteen long chapters of direct, circumstantial narrative, as concrete as in *Mice and Men*. People in definite settings talk and act, and the implications of their sayings and doings are left—in these chapters—to the reader. But alternating with these are fifteen short chapters, amounting to about a seventh of the book, which generalize the experiences of the central characters and put them in a wide setting of time and space, of human needs and hopes beset by social and economic forces.

The Joad clan, eleven of them, are evicted from the Oklahoma farm where they have been sharecropping in the dust-bowl. Allured by handbills they swarm out to the California fruit and cotton country in an army of vagrants so large that it cheapens the labor market to the point where they face starving without work or working on starvation wages. They frighten the Californians as undesirable aliens, and branded as Reds they are so mistreated that their latter end is harsher than their first. The little clan is depleted by deaths and defections. The elder men lose hope and stamina, the children grow up wild, the maturing sons and daughter are poisoned by the grapes of wrath. Tom, the older son, who has already served a term for killing a man in self-defense, slays another in mad rage at him as an official agent of injustice. The mother of the family holds out in the desperate certainty that she is needed by all the others, canny, long-suffering, sympathetic, coercive, defiantly brutal as occasion demands, but endlessly dependable. And over all rules the tyranny of the skies. The book begins in a drought and ends with a flood.

This is the surface story. The linking passages form a series of prose equivalents for mural paintings or sketches for them. They offer Steinbeck's interpretation of the frontier, an enlargement of the post-pioneering period and a retracing of the "slow steps that made the movement" comparable to the steps in the crossing of the continent. The share-croppers were driven off the land of which they had become a part by a machine, but the tractor was owned by a company, and the company was controlled by the banks. It was all as impersonal as death. The orchards too were owned by companies controlled by banks, and the little producers who did not scale down their wages with the big ones

John Steinbeck

were crowded out of business. An orchard which could be run by a dozen men for fifty weeks in the year needed a thousand for a fortnight, and the owners menaced the community by drawing in two men for every job and resenting their presence beyond their term of work. On every side the migrants suffered hardship and imposed it on each other in the dire struggle for survival. Toward the middle of the book, in one of these generalized passages, Steinbeck states his theme and suggests a reply to those who condemn the book because it is brutal and coarse or vilify it as a sensational piece of vicious propaganda.

"The western land, nervous under the beginning change. The Western States, nervous as horses before a thunder storm. The great owners, nervous, sensing a change, knowing nothing of the nature of change. The great owners, striking at the immediate thing, the widening government, the growing labor unity; striking at new taxes, at plans; not knowing these things are results, not causes. . . . . The causes lie deep and simply—the causes are a hunger in a stomach, multiplied a million times; a hunger in a single soul, hunger for joy and some security, multiplied a million times; muscles and mind aching to grow, to work, to create, multiplied a million times. The last clear, definite function of man—muscles aching to work, minds aching to create beyond the single need—this is man. To build a wall, to build a house, a dam, and in the wall and house and dam to put something of Manself, and to Manself to take back something of the wall, the house, the dam; to take hard muscles from the lifting, to take the clear lines and form from conceiving. For man, unlike any other thing organic or inorganic in the universe, grows beyond his work, walks up the stairs of his concepts, emerges ahead of his accomplishments.''

So much for the tale and the moral. As to the materials of it, the annals of the poor are no longer short and simple in the complex twentieth century. They could be short and simple only when a clan, attached to one locality, could live in one drab set of circumstances from generation to generation; when eviction meant only eviction from one poor hovel to another a little poorer within a day's tramping. But when the industrial picture is magnified a thousand fold in numbers and distances, it is also a thousand fold complicated. William Godwin was once concerned with political justice in the eighteenth century. When he stated his theme in the form of a novel he made Caleb Williams the victim of one bad man in one limited countryside. When John Steinbeck contemplates injustice a hundred and fifty years later, he makes an agrarian populace, flung over a million square miles, the victims of an economic system in a machine age.

John Steinbeck

The Joads are coarsened and brutalized by the conditions that overwhelm them. Their words and actions reveal this. Something has happened to the twentieth-century reading public too. Literature is no longer censored for the gentle reader, no longer demands elegance as an accompaniment to clearness and force. So ugly words and ugly facts can be printed in these latter years, and for the most part only ugly minds resent them; for the gentle reader of today distinguishes between the things represented and the writer who describes them and resents only ugliness and dirtiness in the author. This is an elusive truth, but it is nonetheless true. The proof of it lies in the fact that the gentle reader recognizes the coarse and ugly diction of the Joads as a part of their external selves and sees that beneath this and under their skins they are quite as human and admirable as any bookful of characters from Henry James or Mrs. Wharton. Casy, the ex-preacher, who often speaks for the author, explains, "Maybe you wonder about me using bad words. Well, they ain't bad to me no more. They're just words folks use, and they don't mean nothing bad with 'em." The ungentle readers, who decry the ugliness in the book, simply betray a high selective attention to that aspect of it. It would be a waste of time to answer them statistically, but I open to twenty scattered pages quite at random and find five bits of profanity and one Elizabethan piece of ribaldry, in total a little fraction of one page.

Casy is a seeker for truth. He goes into the wilderness and finds truth in his heart. The love of God is the love of mankind. "Maybe that's the Holy Sperit—the human sperit—the whole shebang. Maybe all men got one big soul ever'body's got a part of." This is transcendentalism, and it is pure Christianity. Casy carries his belief to the uttermost and lays down his life for his friends. Tom Joad, ex-convict, can understand Casy. He is a good son and brother. He is through with hating as a motive in life, almost altogether through with it except as it is momentarily roused by an insult or a blow. Like Caleb Williams, he is badgered into being a fugitive from justice. "Ma" Joad is a strong citadel. "Imperturbability could be depended upon, and from her great and humble position in the family she had taken a dignity and a clean, calm beauty. From her position as healer her hands had become sure and cool and quiet; from her position as arbiter she had become as remote and faultless in judgment as a goddess." So Steinbeck introduces her; so she remains till the end.

Grapes of Wrath became a culmination and a compendium of Steinbeck. All it contains was clearly indicated in his earlier works: the primitive passions—lust, fear, hatred, greed, cruelty; the elemental virtues—love, reverence, loyalty, benevolence, attachment to the soil, delight in craftsmanship. The range of characters is wide, and nobility appears in humble guises. The underlying "philosophy" is the philosophy stated at the outset in *The Cup of Gold*—that no good can come to the man who cannot tell dross from gold. Steinbeck is, after all, a good deal of an evangelist. No wonder that in his most ambitious work his evangelism is most evident. Critics who deal with his latest work alone can miss the point quite as completely as snap-judgment readers. It is beside the point for conservatives and standpatters to scold at the propagandist effect of the book. Prosperous California is angry; oddly enough, Oklahoma does not seem to be. Localities have always berated the writers who have written frankly about them. But California and Oklahoma, peach- and cotton-picking, are incidental to Steinbeck. What he is concerned with are the human hungers for food, for joy, for security, multiplied a million times and a million times frustrated, and with the human spirit persistent through the travail of social change to fulfil the ends that can be attained only in the realization that there is "one big soul ever'body's got a part of."

XV
Knowledge and Wisdom

NEARING the end of forty years in the study and teaching of literary history, I find myself thinking back along the changes that have taken place in the relations of the arts and the sciences.

Two scientists first made me aware of what was going on. One was a biologist, and no mean one, whom I encountered one early autumn day on the steps of the Boston Public Library. We were there on our particular jobs and happened to meet at lunch time on the conversational no-man's-land between our fields of interest. We parted feeling that the talk had been good—but just after we had turned our backs on one another he called me for a final word. "You literary fellows make me tired," he said. "We scientists go along working week after week, and year after year; and finally we arrive at something like a truth. Then we turn around and find that some doggone poet has said it all before."

The other was a physicist, a later Nobel prize winner. In those days he used now and then to come out from the laboratory for a breathing spell; and

one afternoon as we were watching a tennis match
he turned on me to express his wonder that any intelligent man could spend his life in the pursuit of
literature when he might be working in physics. He
did not say it to be offensive, and he did not say it to
be funny. It was simply his way of saying that he
and his kind were dealing with the tangibles, that
they could determine the speed of light within one
per cent of one per cent of one per cent, while we who
were no scientists could know no exactness, follow
no method, reach no verifiable results, never be anything but speculative agnostics who dealt in irresponsible allegations about everything in general
and nothing in particular. And the fact is that when
he said what he did and implied what he did I felt,
at first thought, that he had me. I did not know the
answer; could not find one. After second thought,
too, and a reading of such books of popularized science as Slosson's *Creative Chemistry* and Russell's
ABC of the Atom (for this was long before the day
of Jeans and Eddington and Whitehead), I stood
reconvicted. I and all my kind were hopeless ama-
teurs.

I would have stayed in the abyss reserved for victims of inferiority complexes if two saving things
had not happened. First was the discovery that,
while all scientists seemed superior to all humanists,
there was a hierarchy among them, a stratification

of pharisaisms. At the top were physicists and chemists. They had their data pretty well simplified. They had found new names for the elder four elements—earth, air, fire, and water. They called them solids, liquids, gases, and energy now and had subdivided them into groups and series. They even had prospective additions, like new faculty appointees who had not yet reported but whose names and traits were well known, so that they would be recognized when they turned up. All the elements that were on the job had been reduced to molecules and atoms, and they were beginning to talk about electrons and ions and photons and neutrons. Everything seemed to be in order. Moreover, the physicists had another matter well in hand. That was control of experimentation. Control in physics is like an executive session of an administrative body in an air-conditioned room. All visitors are barred, all conditions are fixed—pressure, temperature, humidity—and the experiment, or the discussion, comes out right because every factor is exactly known. It leads to a kind of complacency common to corporation directors and physical scientists.

As I looked around among my colleagues I could see that that was why the physicist was such a pharisee toward the biological scientist. The physicist thanked God that he was not as the biologist was, because the biologist did not have such neat data or such experimental control; he never could be safe against an uninvited microbe or bacillus. This made him, scientifically speaking, rather promiscuous, to be looked down upon by the ultra-respectable. However, the biologist had his compensations and was quick to accept them. He looked down with even greater scorn on the social scientist, the pseudo-scientist who was dealing with the most elusive of all indeterminables, the human factor, sometimes misleadingly referred to as the human equation. The social scientist could pile up his statistics mountain high, but not all the graphs and charts in Arabia could purify that little band. They were far down in the caste system. So in the logic of events there was but one course for them. Caught redhanded, they could pour out the vials of contempt on the sole remaining group, the humanists, who dealt with history, religion, philosophy, and the arts.

This, happily, was one thing to give the humanist courage—science did not present an unbroken front. Some point in the line must be vulnerable. And a second reassurance was that the physicists promptly left an opening which was caused by their lack of charity. Charity, you will remember, is not puffed up, doth not behave itself unseemly; and charity proveth all things. But the physicist, after getting the whole world of matter into a test tube, seemed

(261)

to be bored by the simplicity of his problems and began to reach out into infinitude, on the one hand, and infinitesimality, on the other. These excursions naturally restored a sporting interest to physical science, but it also transformed the sporting scientist into an odd combination of poet, metaphysician, and religious mystic. Not being able to measure infinity, he could yet tell us with a sober face that it has a shape; it is a bent ellipse. Not being able to measure the infinitesimal, he could tell us that the realms of the quanta are the realms of energiastic monism.

You can hardly imagine what a reassurance this energiastic monism gave the humanist. But you must take it from me that the moment the scientist had turned metaphysician and mystic he was ready to roost on the same bough with the man of letters. "Come on up," said the humanist. "There's lots of room. Let's take a little speculative flight together. This reminds me of a remark a biologist once made to me." And he could not now be rebuffed when the physicist replied, "You leave hypotheses to me. I'm trained; I am the only one who knows how to use them." For the obvious answer was, "Go back to your laboratory with your curved ellipse, if you can get it in, and your energiastic monism; and just leave the old common and garden varieties of hypotheses about faith and hope and charity, and goodness and beauty and truth to me." Thus the humanist, so meek a quarter of a century ago, fulfils the scripture, "Blessed is the meek, for he shall inherit the earth."

As a result of our ups and downs, we nonscientists, as we enjoy our restored rights to life, liberty, and the pursuit of truth, are well aware of dangers and duties.

The dangers, which particularly threaten the newer recruits to academia, are the temptations to play scientist with only a parade of method or with subjects which do not submit to scientific treatment. They crop up every little while. Not so long ago, for instance, there was a period of solemn pedantry on the subject of versification. People were writing books on the science of English verse and making the subject as intricate as possible by adopting a set of technical polysyllabic terms and imposing them on a set of doubtful assumptions. They wanted us, for example, to believe, or pretend, of the youthful Bryant, the seventeen-year-old boy of the Berkshire Mountains, that when he wrote

> So live, that when thy summons comes to join
> The innumerable caravan, which moves
> To that mysterious realm, where each shall take
> His chamber in the silent halls of death,

he took out a contract to write regular iambic pentameter and not to depart from it without some sort of poetical dispensation. And then, because like all good poets he did continually depart from it, the prosodists labored to explain that he was *consistently* inconsistent, and they named the variations—they were poetical sins—syncope, synaeresis, synecdoche, synezesis, and the like; so that when Bryant wrote a line that was not perfectly regular, they contended that his theory was quite all right and that his execution could be technically condoned, like the conduct of a sound theologian who indulges in minor lapses from grace. Today we are less given to trying to explain away the rival claims of the pattern rhythm and the spoken word; and we are simpler and more honest. With the result, incidentally, that poetry has a better chance to survive the classroom.

Lately, for another example, the new realm of psychoanalysis has been disclosed to a startled world. The explorers are still establishing its outlines. But the exploiters as always have rushed in too. Some of them, physicotherapists with little knowledge, less scruples, and great enterprise, have reaped a rich harvest from private practice. And some literary folk, who knew even less than the pseudo-scientist exploiters, have reveled in chances for speculation that biography has seemed to offer. Starting with ignorance and a few pat formulas and proceeding with insufficient data—not even aware that the data the scientist relies on with the living subject are forever closed to the examiner of posthumous documents—these literary dabblers have held high carnival in the make-believe diagnosis of writers who invited sensational interpretations and often have been seriously regarded by a gullible public. Moreover, collaborations between scientist and critic have fallen down, partly through mutual ignorance of each other's material and partly through the fact that the scientist has usually overawed the critic and led him to subscribe to portentous nonsense. For it often happens, through a nice play of compensation, that the scientist away from his laboratory can outdo the rawest amateur in the fantastic irresponsibility of his conclusions.

Even at that it is not easy to surpass the student of letters at this if the literary man has come to distrust his own procedures and feels that he must vindicate himself by a show of scientific method. Letters includes, of course, the provinces of language, of the process of writing, and of the study of the written product. The sister subjects of language and speech submit to scientific study. Jakob Grimm was a great philologian, and Grimm's law of phonetic change is just as valid as Newton's, Kepler's, or Mendel's laws and just as intricate. But it is another story outside the fields of linguistics and phonetics. Yet I have seen teachers of elementary composition approach their task with all the grimness of Grimm, apparently committed to the idea that a hapless beginner cannot be intrusted with a complex declarative sentence unless he is first made a master of logic. I have heard teachers of elementary courses in literature maintain that beginners could not possibly face a page of a dozen declarative sentences without a careful grounding in dialectic. They have seemed to feel that a page of print, even the most innocent and lucid page, was an intricate web of enigmas with a fell spirit as its center, lurking under some subordinate clause, ready to dart out and bewilder the unwary.

And at the other far extreme of the scholastic course I once met a pair of scholars who, when asked the objective of their scholarship, replied that its primary function was to do what they called establishing texts, by which they meant reproducing the original versions of great works of literature, with scrupulous regard to all archaic spellings and misspellings, discarded systems of punctuation, and typographical errors, which first had to be meticulously printed and then meticulously corrected in footnotes. This was to be their contribution to contemporary culture.

I do not think lightly of the need for knowing just what an author has written; of the way he writes if he be a poet, or novelist, or dramatist, of

the manner of man he is or once was, if this knowledge throws light on his writings; or of striving for
a firm grasp of what he has committed to print. I
just discount the parade of scientific method when it
turns out to be no more than a pretense of science by
the unscientific.

And this leads to what the man of letters may do
for science and all learning. As I have suggested,
speaking of prosody, there is a tendency in this age
of special eruditions to split the language up into
dialects filled with technical hairsplitters. Some of
these are exact and necessary; sometimes they are
even compact, most often in the biological and
physical sciences. Some are old words used in new
ways, nouns for verbs, like the sociologist's *to orient*,
or the political scientist's *to implement*. Some have
mysterious and beneficent properties and are spoken
with an air of incantation, like *integration* and *cor-
relation*. All have their justification when employed
with economy by speakers qualified to use them.
But they put a kind of spell on academic novices,
just as slang or mild profanity do on the pre-adoles-
cent or new terms suddenly become current do on
you and me. Words, for instance, like *camouflage* in
1917. Camouflage, we discovered, meant a method
of disguising an object so that it looked as if it were
not there. A lot of this extravagance of technicality
on the lips of the lazy and the unscrupulous is a sort

set by the forces of destruction that science has let loose. It is to restore a common faith in the things that are more excellent, a faith which, if it only be based on beliefs that are valid and vital, can actually *become* the substance of things hoped for, the evidence of things not seen.

Index

Index

America in Contemporary Fiction